Hey Glamour Girl!

This book is written for girls just like you who want to be in style from head to toe! You will discover all the basics that make up your style, such as beauty, fashion, and character. From **hair, make-up,** and **nails,** to **hats, skirts, jeans,** and **tees,** you will have fun discovering your personal style, and embracing who you are as God's girl!

And guess what? I'll let you in on a little secret: you are unique! **Nobody else looks like you.** God has made you to be **YOU!** You are the only one with your body, eyes, hair, likes, and dislikes. You truly have your own style!

Have you ever wondered what the Bible says about all of this?

Colossians 3:12-17 tells us what God thinks is stylish: compassion, humility, gentleness, and patience, to name a few things. *The Christian Girl's Guide to Style* will walk you through Scripture, and give you fun fashion facts, activities, and style tips that will help you discover who God made you to be! **What are you waiting for?**

Chapter 1

What is Style?

Yet, O LORD, you are our Father. We are the clay,
you are the potter; we are all the work of your hand.

~ Isaiah 64:8

Uniquely You! ✿

Zoë looked in the mirror and frowned. Getting dressed for school had become a chore. Not only were her pants too short, but so was her T-shirt. She must have grown three inches in the past month; she needed a new wardrobe. Her mom had promised to take her shopping on Saturday, but Saturday wasn't soon enough.

Zoë grabbed a long tank top to put under her T-shirt and slipped on a pair of sandals, hoping these touches would make her look like she was wearing capris. Zoë took a final glance in the mirror, shrugged in defeat, and continued getting ready. After gobbling down a bowl of cereal, she ran back upstairs to brush her teeth and grab a headband to keep her bangs from falling in her eyes. She turned at the sound of her friend's car in the driveway.

"Zoë, your ride's here!" her mom called from the bottom of the stairs.

Zoë snatched her backpack and ran down the stairs to meet her carpool. "Bye Mom!" she called and headed out the front door, accidentally slamming it on the way out.

"Hey Zoë," said Rebecca. "Hop in."

Zoë waved and took a seat. Rebecca had been her friend since the first grade. Their friendship had had its ups and downs in the past, but this year they were close.

"Zoë, you look taller to me these days," said Rebecca's mom. "Have you grown?"

"Yeah, three inches," Zoë said dismissively. She didn't want to be reminded.

Once Zoë was belted in, she noticed the cute pants and T-shirt her friend was wearing. "New clothes?" she asked.

"Yeah," Rebecca replied. "My mom went shopping the other day. You should see the pile of clothes she bought!"

"Wow, must be nice," Zoë said as she tugged on the bottom of her T-shirt.

"There was a big sale…you know how my mom is when there's a sale," Rebecca said, smiling.

"My mom's taking me shopping on Saturday," Zoë replied, reaching into her backpack and taking out a banana. "She told me she had a growth spurt when she was my age." Zoë peeled the banana and took a bite.

"I wish I would grow," said Rebecca, sitting up straighter in her seat. "I think I'm the shortest one in our class."

"Yeah, but if you grew, your new clothes would be too short," Zoë said. She looked down at her pants with a sigh.

"I've never noticed your clothes being short," Rebecca said laughing. "You always look cool. I like the way you dress. And you never know, you may start a new trend."

"Thanks," said Zoë, feeling a bit more confident. She tucked the banana peel into her lunch bag and grabbed her hairbrush.

"I've always wanted long blonde hair like yours instead of my curly brown hair," Rebecca told Zoë, blowing at a stray curl.

"Really?" Zoë said. She ran the brush once through her straight hair, pushed her headband in place, and tossed the brush back in her backpack. "I've always thought it would be fun to have your curly hair."

Rebecca's mom pulled up to the curb in front of the school. "Have a great day, you two," she said.

"Thanks for the ride," Zoë said as she opened the door, grabbed her backpack, and slid out of the van.

"Bye Mom," said Rebecca, following Zoë out the door.

"I guess we all come in different shapes and sizes," Zoë said. "God made me tall and you short. He made you with curly hair and He made me with straight hair." Zoë gazed at the other girls entering the school. "Why do we always want what others have?"

"I don't know," Rebecca replied, pulling up the handle on her rolling backpack. "But I'm glad that God made us all different."

"Yeah," sighed Zoë. "Otherwise, we'd all look alike. But still, I wouldn't mind having her outfit," Zoë said, motioning to a girl walking into the school.

"Come on, before we're late," Rebecca said, laughing. The girls linked arms and sprinted to class.

What Do You Think?

Think about a time when you felt frustrated with how you looked. How did it make you feel?

_____

_____

_____

_____

Do you ever wish you looked like your friends? Or a famous celebrity?

_____

_____

_____

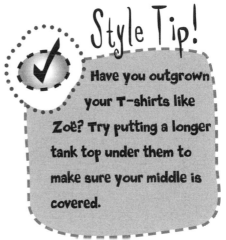

Style Tip!

Have you outgrown your T-shirts like Zoë? Try putting a longer tank top under them to make sure your middle is covered.

Do you know that God made you just the way He wanted you to look, with _your_ hair, eyes, and body? How does that make you feel?

_____

_____

_____

_____

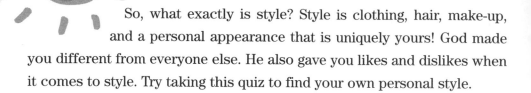

Try It!   Style Quiz:

So, what exactly is style? Style is clothing, hair, make-up, and a personal appearance that is uniquely yours! God made you different from everyone else. He also gave you likes and dislikes when it comes to style. Try taking this quiz to find your own personal style.

1. What type of jewelry expresses your style the best?
   a. Lots of jewelry, the more the better
   b. Jewelry? What jewelry?
   c. A single necklace
   d. Colorful earrings with a matching necklace
   e. What everyone else is wearing

2. What type of shoes express your personality the best?
   a. Shoes that express ME, with creative shoelaces or pins
   b. Tennis shoes
   c. Mary Janes or loafers
   d. Brightly colored sandals
   e. The new style of the season

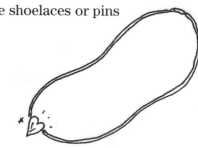

3. How do you usually wear your hair?
   a. With lots of barrettes, scrunchies, and clips
   b. In a ponytail
   c. Down, with a headband
   d. In braids, or ponytails, or up in a twist
   e. The way my favorite TV star wears it

4. What do you wear on Saturdays?
   a. The same clothes I wear at school
   b. Shorts and a T-shirt
   c. A sweater and cuffed jeans
   d. A T-shirt I got on vacation and my favorite flowered capris
   e. Anything comfortable, as long as it looks good

_. How do you describe how you like to dress?

   a. Layers with my own flair

   b. Sweatshirts and jeans

   c. Button-down sweaters

   d. Bright colors

   e. Whatever is the latest at the mall

If you circled mostly:

a: You are HIP. You are aware of what's going on in the fashion world, but you still want your own style.

B: You are SPORTY. You are the athletic type. You are not fussy when it comes to clothes and you'd rather be playing outside than dealing with your hair or jewelry. Your tennis shoes are the most important part of your wardrobe.

C: You are CLASSY. You like things simple with your hair, jewelry, and the way you dress. Crisp and clean describes you and your clothes. You enjoy wearing skirts with button-down shirts and you may have pennies in your loafers.

D: You are CUTE. You enjoy colorful things when it comes to your wardrobe. T-shirts, fun capri pants with stripes or flowers, and sweaters with colorful buttons are in your closet and drawers.

E: You are TRENDY. You love to shop and update your wardrobe at least a few times a year. You must have the latest style when it comes to your clothes and usually don't outgrow anything. You love to look at magazines to see what you should wear, and your friends call you and ask for advice.

Did you know?

Bodies come in many different shapes, sizes, and colors. Did you know that what you eat and how you exercise is only part of the equation? The other part is in your family genes. Take a look at your parents. That will help you determine what you might look like when you're fully grown. But remember, your body type is uniquely yours!

Fashion Tip: Wear clothes that are comfortable and make you feel good about your body. Play up your best features. Clothes that are too baggy or too tight will not enhance your unique appearance.

Ask Kelsey!

Q: I went shopping the other day with my friend and her mom. We both tried on the same top and skirt. My friend looked great. I didn't. Why?

A: Since we all come in different shapes and sizes, clothes look different on different people:

Tall and thin—you probably look best in wide belts, and skirts that are not too short or too long. You can wear your tops a little longer over your skirts or pants.

Short and small—wear slim, narrow belts and clothes that are more fitted. Pick fabric that is soft and flowing with a nice fit. Stay away from big designs—they can be overwhelming for smaller figures.

Curvy—you can wear clothes with stripes that go up and down, but not across. Wear dresses and skirts just below the knee and tops that curve in a bit at the waist.

Q: I have the jealousy bug. Some of my friends have the cutest things— like earrings, hair accessories, hoodies, and jeans. Why do I always compare myself with others?

A: When we compare ourselves with others, it really means that we're not confident in our unique style. We want what others have because we think they have it all together. Chances are, your friends want something someone else has, too. The Bible talks about being content with what God has given us (check out Hebrews 13:5). Contentment is hard to grasp, even as an adult—ask your mom or dad. But when we ask God to help us, He can give us the confidence we need to be ourselves and be happy with what we have.

Q: The other day, my mom told me to change my clothes. She didn't like the way I was dressed. She said my skirt was too short and my T-shirt was too tight. I want to look like my friends. How am I going to have my own personal style if my mom won't let me?

A: Do you really have your own personal style if you want to dress like your friends? Sometimes girls pressure each other into dressing alike to feel a part of the group. And sometimes friends want us to do things that we know our parents don't agree with—like wearing short skirts and tight T-shirts. It's best to sit down with your parents and talk about what is appropriate and what's not. Your mom was a girl once and understands the pressures of fitting in. Maybe you can start a new trend: one that shows your unique style and your inward beauty.

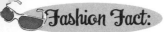

Fashion Fact:

In the 1700's, children's clothing changed from looking like a miniature version of adult clothing to clothing made just for children.

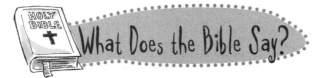

What Does the Bible Say?

And why do you worry about clothes? See how the lilies of the field grow. They do not labor or spin. Yet I tell you that not even Solomon in all his splendor was dressed like one of these. If that is how God clothes the grass of the field, which is here today and tomorrow is thrown into the fire, will he not much more clothe you, O you of little faith?

~ Matthew 6:28-30

I also want women to dress modestly, with decency and propriety, not with braided hair or gold or pearls or expensive clothes, but with good deeds, appropriate for women who profess to worship God.

~ 1 Timothy 2:9-10

Your beauty should not come from outward adornment, such as braided hair and the wearing of gold jewelry and fine clothes. Instead, it should be that of your inner self, the unfading beauty of a gentle and quiet spirit, which is of great worth in God's sight.   *~ 1 Peter 3:3-4*

Therefore, as God's chosen people, holy and dearly loved, clothe yourselves with compassion, kindness, humility, gentleness and patience. Bear with each other and forgive whatever grievances you may have against one another. Forgive as the Lord forgave you. And over all these virtues put on love, which binds them all together in perfect unity.

Let the peace of Christ rule in your hearts, since as members of one body you were called to peace. And be thankful. Let the word of Chri.. dwell in you richly as you teach and admonish one another with all wisdom, and as you sing psalms, hymns and spiritual songs with gratitude in your hearts to God. And whatever you do, whether in word or deed, do it all in the name of the Lord Jesus, giving thanks to God the Father through Him.

~ Colossians 3:12-17

✉ Letters to God

Hi, God! It's me, Zoë! Well, Mom and I went shopping on Saturday. It was fun. I tried on all sorts of cool clothes. At first, every pair of pants I tried on fit in the waist, but came up to my ankles. Then, when I tried on pants that were long enough, the waist was too big.

Mom saved the day by finding me the cutest black belt with hearts on it! We bought some cute T-shirts, too, in all sorts of colors. My favorite one is pink with a cool pattern on it. After we went shopping, I decided I liked being tall. I think it was because of the cute belt.

On the way home, we stopped for frozen yogurt. As we were eating, Mom said, "You have the prettiest hair." And to think I wanted Rebecca's curly hair. It looks good on her, but I'm glad mine is straight. I licked my yogurt, smiled, and said, "Thanks, Mom."

Then Mom said, "But, more importantly, you're beautiful on the inside."

I took the last bite of my cone, wiped my mouth on a napkin, and gave my mom a hug.

So, anyway, I forgot what else I was going to say, so I'm going to bed now. Talk to you later.

Love, —Me

Now, it's your turn. Write your own letter to God and tell Him about a time you needed to show compassion to someone else.

_____

_____

_____

_____

_____

_____

_____

_____

_____

_____

_____

_____

_____

_____

_____

_____

_____

_____

_____

_____

_____

_____

Make It!

Floating Bead Necklace

While making this necklace, think about how God made you just the way you are!

✳ What you need:

- ♡ Scissors
- ♡ Fishing line
- ♡ 2 clamshell bead tips
- ♡ Needle-nose pliers
- ♡ Barrel clasp
- ♡ Translucent glass or plastic beads using some or all of the colors below. These colors represent:
  - ✳ Pink – Compassion
  - ✳ Light blue – Kindness
  - ✳ Yellow – Humility
  - ✳ Green – Gentleness
  - ✳ Lavender – Patience
  - ✳ Clear – Forgiveness
  - ✳ Red – Love
  - ✳ White – Peace
  - ✳ Orange – Thankfulness
  - ✳ Dark blue – Wisdom

❊ What you do:

Cut a piece of the fishing line 36 inches long. String a bead onto the line, then loop the fishing line back through the bead to hold the bead in place. Add the rest of the beads, spacing them evenly throughout the necklace.

Insert the end of the fishing line into a clamshell bead tip and tie a double knot to keep the beads from slipping off.

Using the pliers, pinch the clamshell bead tip and attach the barrel clasp. Now you have a colorful necklace that perfectly expresses your personality!

Memory Verse:

Write down the memory verse from the beginning of the chapter. Memorize it. Think about how God created you to be special and unique.

_____

_____

_____

❀ Takeaway Thought:

As you look in the mirror, think about how God made you. What color hair do you have? What color eyes? What do you like about how you look? Name five things. God made you the way you are…special and unique.

🙏 Prayer:

Thank you, Lord, for making me, ME! Help me to be positive about the way I look and to be glad that I'm unique. You are an awesome God. In Jesus' name, Amen.

Chapter 2

Stepping Out

An anxious heart weighs a man down,
but a kind word cheers him up.
~ Proverbs 12:25

Emma's New Sandals

Emma ran to the school bus just in time. Her alarm clock had failed to go off this morning and she was running late—so late, she almost missed the bus. She had, however, taken time to put on her new sandals, which made her feel like she would fit right in at school. Emma tripped up the stairs of the bus and grabbed the handrail as she swung her backpack up on her shoulder.

"Nice catch," said the bus driver, giving Emma a great big smile. "New sandals?"

Wow, even the bus driver noticed! Emma thought. "Yeah," she responded.

"Be careful getting off the bus when we get to school," said the bus driver. He winked and pulled the handle, closing the door.

"Thanks," said Emma in a monotone voice. *How embarrassing. Strike one for the cute new sandals.* Emma quickly found a seat toward the front.

"Hey Emma," said her friend Hannah sitting a couple of rows behind her. "What are you doing sitting up there? Come sit by me."

"Okay," Emma said. She hoped no one had noticed her embarrassing entrance.

The bus stopped and Emma quickly moved two rows back to sit by her friend. "Cute sandals!" Hannah gushed, leaning over to take a closer look.

"Thanks," Emma smiled. "I bought them with my own money. My mom said they were a want, not a need, so I had to buy them myself."

"Hey, did you see that girl's shoes sitting across from us?" whispered Hannah. "Aren't they the ugliest shoes you've ever seen?"

"They sure aren't pretty to look at," Emma replied as she fidgeted with the strap of her backpack. "Her mom probably wouldn't buy her sandals either."

"Her mom just needs to buy her normal shoes," said Hannah a bit too loudly. The brown-haired girl looked over at them and slid her feet under the seat. "Oops," said Hannah.

Emma felt Hannah's elbow digging into her side. Emma dug her elbow back into Hannah's side. The two girls looked at each other and burst into giggles. Emma knew she was wrong to laugh, but she couldn't help it. She was afraid to look over at the brown-haired girl, knowing they had hurt her feelings.

The bus came to a stop. They were at school.

Emma quickly grabbed her heavy backpack and made her way to the door. She grabbed the handrail so she wouldn't trip making her exit, and climbed the three steps down and off the bus. Emma, thinking Hannah was right behind her, turned around, and came face to face with the brown-haired girl. "Uh-oh. Uh, hi," Emma stuttered. She didn't know what else to do.

"Your sandals are so pretty," said the girl.

"Thanks." Emma looked at the ground as they both walked up the front stairs leading to the school. "What's your name?"

"Jessica," the girl replied.

"Look, my friend and I were joking around on the bus. I hope we didn't hurt your feelings," Emma said. "And by the way, my name is Emma."

"No," said Jessica. "It's OK."

Emma turned to face her. "No, it's not OK. I feel really bad," she said. Emma bit her lower lip and glanced at her watch. "You know, your shoes would look really cute with some pink shoelaces," she said.

"You think so?" Jessica's eyes widened.

"I know so," said Emma, smiling. "In fact, my mom just bought me a few new pairs for my tennis shoes. Why don't I bring you a pair tomorrow?"

"Thanks," Jessica said, smiling back.

See you later on the bus," Emma said as Hannah approached.

"Bye." Jessica waved and walked away.

"What was that all about?" asked Hannah.

"Just trying to make things right," Emma told her friend, climbing t̶ steps of the school two at a time. "Let's hurry so we won't be late to class."

"Don't trip," said Hannah.

"We all trip-up sometimes," Emma said with a grin.

What Do You Think? ???

Do you think that Emma will be more careful about what she says the next time? Why? _____

_____

_____

Have you ever said something you wished you could take back? How could you have handled the situation differently?

_____

_____

_____

How can you show kindness to someone who needs it today?

_____

_____

_____

_____

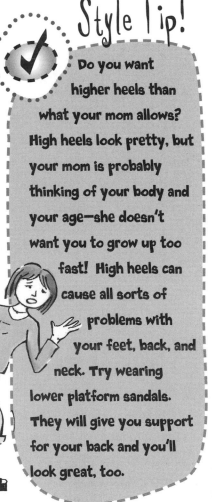

Style Tip!

Do you want higher heels than what your mom allows? High heels look pretty, but your mom is probably thinking of your body and your age—she doesn't want you to grow up too fast! High heels can cause all sorts of problems with your feet, back, and neck. Try wearing lower platform sandals. They will give you support for your back and you'll look great, too.

Hidden Word Puzzle

Try It!

Find the hidden words and hidden message in this word puzzle. *Puzzle answers appear at the back of the book.*

Z	L	O	V	S	L	S	Y	S	H	B	A	G	H	S
C	W	O	W	O	E	P	T	N	Y	E	O	Q	I	R
M	I	G	V	S	S	O	X	N	P	D	G	N	G	E
G	T	V	G	Y	O	L	H	W	I	Q	J	Y	H	F
A	A	O	E	B	E	F	A	S	V	H	M	A	H	A
O	L	Q	N	U	L	P	K	D	S	U	H	X	E	O
C	Z	I	L	S	X	I	P	D	N	I	O	A	E	L
O	A	R	X	K	N	L	J	J	I	A	N	P	L	O
R	P	L	D	D	S	F	K	O	H	U	S	N	S	R
S	R	E	P	P	I	L	S	R	N	T	H	Q	E	N
S	T	A	L	F	A	N	I	R	E	L	L	A	B	T
J	S	P	C	M	A	R	Y	J	A	N	E	S	J	T
U	Z	P	N	J	Z	T	T	Q	I	F	H	R	J	X
Y	U	L	Y	H	N	A	Z	E	B	B	D	C	L	T
A	A	I	G	B	J	C	Z	E	G	U	X	N	C	V

Hidden words:

BALLERINA FLATS
CLOGS
FLIP FLOPS
HIGH HEELS

LOAFERS
MARY JANES
RAINBOOTS

SANDALS
SLIPPERS
TENNIS SHOES

29

Did you know?

Wearing new shoes or sandals is a lot of fun, but if they don't fit properly, you can get blisters or sore spots that really hurt. So, what should you do to make sure your shoes fit well? Make sure you have both feet measured every time you buy a new pair of shoes or sandals. Try the shoes on and walk around the store to make sure they don't pinch or rub. It's fun to have the latest style, but comfort will keep your feet happy and healthy.

Fashion Tip: Time to throw out those stinky tennis shoes? Make sure when you buy your next pair that they are made from breathable materials, such as leather or canvas. Your feet will stay cooler and dryer and they will smell better, too!

Ask Kelsey!

Q: I have bigger feet than my mom and sister. I have a hard time finding cute shoes in my size. Will I ever stop growing? Help!

A: A lot of girls these days have bigger feet than their moms. In fact, most women's feet are bigger now than when your mom was younger. You've got to love your feet no matter what their size. Without them, it would be hard to walk, run, or ride a bike! It's difficult to know when your feet will stop growing, but don't worry—they will.

As for finding cute shoes in your size, keep searching. You'll find exactly what you're looking for if you're patient. And remember: you can always "jazz" up your shoes by adding cute laces.

Q: I don't know what type of shoe to wear with which clothes. Does it really matter?

A: Of course you have your own sense of style, but here are some suggestions to look your best:

Ankle boots—these look great with long skirts and tights, skirts just above the knee, or pants.

Ballerina flats—these look adorable with Capri pants, leggings, and shorts and skirts at or just above the knee.

Mary Janes—these look stylish with jeans, cords, dresses, and skirts.

Athletic shoes—these should be worn whenever you are exercising or want to feel comfortable.

Rain boots—these keep your feet dry, so make sure you wear them when it's raining outside! Also, make sure they go above your ankle and have plenty of traction on the bottom.

Q: I love shoes! I have pairs in all different colors and styles. My problem is that I can't stop buying them (or asking my parents to.) Is it okay to like shoes so much?

A: Shoes are fun—and fun to wear. Shoes can complete your outfit, help you win a race, or keep your feet warm. But just like anything else, if you put more value on shoes than your relationship with God, you will not be happy. Do you ever wonder why you're not satisfied with the pair of shoes you just bought? They may make you happy for a while, but true happiness doesn't come from material things. Read 1 Timothy 6:7-8 for more on this. Besides, you'll probably outgrow your shoes before you have time to wear them out. Next time you are tempted to buy more shoes, wait until you actually need a pair!

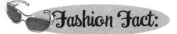

Fashion Fact:

The foot became the focal point of fashion in the 1920's and 30's. Shoe styles were influenced by crazes like the Charleston, a dance that required a shoe with a closed toe and a low heel. In the 1950's and 60's, sandals, ballet slippers, and other casual footwear became fashionable, as pool parties and other outdoor activities became popular.

What Does the Bible Say?

Your word is a lamp to my feet and a light for my path.

~ Psalm 119:105

He who is kind to the poor lends to the LORD, and he will reward him for what he has done.

~ Proverbs 19:17

The LORD appeared to us in the past, saying: "I have loved you with an everlasting love; I have drawn you with loving-kindness."

~ Jeremiah 31:3

I will tell of the kindnesses of the LORD, the deeds for which he is to be praised, according to all the LORD has done for us—yes, the many good things he has done for the house of Israel, according to his compassion and many kindnesses.

~ Isaiah 63:7

"But let him who boasts boast about this: that he understands and knows me, that I am the LORD, who exercises kindness, justice and righteousness on earth, for in these I delight," declares the LORD.

~ Jeremiah 9:24

✉ Letters to God

Hi God, I was so embarrassed yesterday. Besides tripping into the bus (thank goodness only the bus driver noticed), my friend Hannah and I got caught making fun of Jessica's shoes! UGH!

So, last night I dug into my sock drawer and pulled out the three pairs of shoelaces my mom bought for me. I promised Jessica I'd give her a pair to make her shoes look better. I tucked all the shoelaces in my backpack so that she could pick which ones she wanted today on our way to school.

On the bus this morning, I held them out and watched as she looked at them. (I was secretly hoping she wouldn't pick the ones with the flowers.) Of course, she selected the pink shoelaces with the flowers.

I smiled and said, "Good choice."

Jessica quickly slipped out of her shoes and tied on the pretty pink shoelaces just as we pulled into the school parking lot. She grinned at me, grabbed her backpack, and hopped off the bus.

Hannah nudged me and whispered in my ear, "You are the kindest friend anyone could have."

Tonight, my mom hugged me after I told her the story. Thank You, God, for helping me be kind to Jessica and for making things right.

Love, —Emma

Now, it's your turn. Write your own letter to God and tell Him about a time you were kind to someone else.

_____

_____

_____

_____

_____

_____

_____

_____

_____

_____

_____

_____

_____

_____

_____

_____

_____

_____

_____

Make It!

Flowery Flip-Flops

Saying kind words cheers people up! These flowery flip-flops will remind you to be kind.

What you need:

- ♡ Two large silk flowers
- ♡ Scissors or wire cutters
- ♡ Glue gun with glue sticks or craft glue
- ♡ An inexpensive pair of flip-flops (you can purchase these at your local drugstore)

What you do:

Cut the silk flowers off their stems, making sure to keep the flowers intact (a dab of hot glue may be needed to make sure the flowers stay together.) Glue a silk flower to the center of the strap of each flip-flop, where the strap goes between the toes. Allow your flip-flops to dry before wearing them!

Memory Verse:

Write down the memory verse from the beginning of the chapter. Memorize it. Think about how you can be kind to others.

_____

_____

_____

Takeaway Thought:

Being kind to others shows that you are thoughtful of people's feelings and needs. Why not start at home with your family? God delights in showing kindness to you!

Prayer:

Thank You, Lord, that You are kind. Help me to be kind to others. In Jesus' name, Amen.

Chapter 3

Hair, Hair, Hair!

Wait for the LORD;
be strong and take heart
and wait for the LORD.

~ Psalm 27:14

Leah's Haircut

Leah flipped through the fashion magazine looking at all the fun hairstyles. Ponytails, braids, and French twists beckoned her from the pages as she ran her fingers through her short black hair. Leah sighed heavily as she tossed the magazine on the floor. She pulled herself up from her beanbag chair.

"Hey Mom, can I call Felicity?" she asked.

"Yes, but keep it short. I'm expecting a call from your dad in about fifteen minutes."

"All right, I'll tell you when I hang up," Leah replied. She knew her mom never missed a call from her dad when he was away on business. She sat on her parents' bed and picked up the telephone. She noticed a family picture on her mom's dresser. It was taken a few months back when she had long hair. She sighed once again and dialed her friend's phone number.

"Hello?" said Felicity's mom.

"Hi, Mrs. March, this is Leah. Is Felicity home?"

"Yes, I think she's in her room doing homework. Hold on a minute," Mrs. March responded.

Leah could hear Mrs. March's muffled voice calling Felicity. After a couple of minutes, Felicity answered the phone. "Hello?"

"Hey," said Leah. "What are you doing?"

"Oh. Hi, Leah," said Felicity. "Nothing much. What are you doing?"

"Waiting for my hair to grow," Leah said, tugging at the bottom of her short hair.

"Are you still mad at Caleb?" asked Felicity.

"I'm trying not to be," said Leah. "But it's really hard. It took me *forever* to grow my hair long. Why was he chewing gum in school anyway?"

"You should have seen the bubble he made." Felicity giggled. "I've never seen one so big."

"Yeah, I can imagine, because of how much of my hair it ruined. I can believe that one last blow made it fly right out of his mouth and into my hair."

"I almost sat in that chair," said Felicity. "It's not everyday our math teacher lets us sit anywhere we want."

Leah paced the floor as she talked. "I've been ignoring Caleb all week," she said. "I know he feels bad, but he just doesn't understand!"

"I think your hair looks cute," said Felicity. "Maybe you'll start a trend."

"Are *you* going to cut *your* hair short?" Leah asked.

"Well, no," said Felicity.

"I didn't think so," Leah responded. "I'll be graduating high school by the time my hair is long again. How depressing!" Leah stared out her parents' window at the trees in their backyard. "Oh, I'd better get going. My mom's waiting for a phone call from my dad. See you later."

"Bye," said Felicity. "I'll see you tomorrow."

Leah hung up the phone. "I'm off, Mom," she said.

"Thanks, Leah," said Mom. "Can you come down here a minute?"

"Sure," Leah replied. She slowly descended the stairs and joined her mom in the kitchen.

"I wanted you to see what I bought today," Leah's mom said. She reached into a shopping bag and pulled out a magazine. "I thought you might like to see what you can do with short hair."

Leah took the magazine from her mom and glanced at the front cover. She read the titles of the articles: *Short Is In* and *Cute Cuts* popped out at her. She noticed a girl about her age with similar length hair. Leah liked the way the girl had parted it on the side and added a cute clip. She nodded her head in approval. Every page showed girls wearing headbands, clips, or some sort of hair accessory. Leah smiled—she had a whole drawer full of hair supplies.

Leah looked up and saw her mom smiling at her. "What?" Leah asked.

"You noticed, didn't you," Leah's mom replied. "You can still wear all the fun things you like."

The phone rang. Mom would be talking to dad for at least an hour. "I be in my room," mouthed Leah. She tiptoed up the stairs.

Maybe it's time to talk to Caleb, Leah thought. It was an accident, after all. She headed toward the bathroom. She grabbed a hairbrush and brushed her hair with quick strokes. She parted her hair on the side and stuck her favorite butterfly clip in like the girl in the magazine. She smiled at herself in the mirror and headed to her room to start her homework.

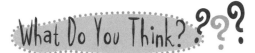

What Do You Think? ???

Why was Leah upset with Caleb?

_____

_____

_____

What do you think Leah said to Caleb the next day at school?

_____

_____

How can you show patience when you have to wait for something?

_____

_____

Style Tip! ✓

For yummy-smelling hair, try this apple rinse. Remember to ask a parent first!

WHAT YOU NEED:
1 large apple, peeled and cut into small pieces
2 tablespoons of apple cider vinegar
2 cups of water

WHAT YOU DO:
Mix together all the ingredients in a blender set on "High." Pour the mixture through a strainer into a clean container. (Throw away the stuff in the strainer.) Pour the contents from the container over your hair after shampooing. Massage through your hair and rinse thoroughly with cool water.

Did you know?

Your hair is made from a type of protein called keratin. A single hair consists of a hair shaft (the part that shows), a root below the skin, and a follicle from which the hair root grows. At the lower end of the follicle is the hair bulb where the hair's color pigment, or melanin, is produced.

 **Fashion Tip:** You may think it would look cool to dye your hair a different color, but having your hair colored or bleached could cause damage that might make the hair break off or fall out temporarily. For now, enjoy the beautiful color God gave you!

Ask Kelsey!

Q: How do I know what type of shampoo and conditioner to use?

A: The most amazing hairstyles start with happy, healthy hair. It's important to find the shampoo and conditioner that are best for your hair, and it's just as important to wash your hair properly. To determine the best shampoo for your hair, you need to figure out what type of hair you have.

If your hair is *oily,* it tends to look stringy if you miss a day of washing. Avoid the word "conditioning" in your shampoo, or else you'll end up with a grease ball for a mane. Instead, look for shampoos with natural ingredients like chamomile, sage oil, or tea tree oil. These ingredients eliminate excess oil without over-drying your strands.

If your hair is *dry,* it tends to be coarse, and maybe curly. Try protein-rich shampoos. Be sure to read the label carefully to make sure protein i. one of the first ingredients.

If your hair is **normal,** it is soft, but not greasy. Your hair can be washed daily or every other day using shampoos for normal hair types that contain a balance of proteins, vitamins, and conditioners to soften your hair without causing build up.

Q: I'm tired of my hair and want a new hairstyle, but I don't know what to do. How do I decide?

A: Finding a new hairstyle can be fun . . . and scary at the same time. The first thing to consider is your face shape:

- ♡ If your face is **round,** your best styles add a little height on top and fall right below your chin. A few layers look great on you, as well as bangs that are long and swept off to the side.
- ♡ If your face is **oval,** you can pull off almost any look: short, long, straight, or wavy. Have fun!
- ♡ If your face is **triangular,** you'll look great in bangs with smooth hair at your jaw line.
- ♡ If your face is a **diamond** shape, you can wear your hair short, with the top layers soft and long, or long with wavy layers by your cheek bones.
- ♡ If your face is **square,** try curly or choppy styles. You'll also look great with long hair with layers that start at your jaw and continue downward.

One of the simplest things you can do before getting your hair cut is to look through magazines for girls your age to get ideas. Keep in mind your face shape. Cut out your favorite styles and then bring them to your hairdresser, who will help you decide if that's the best style for you.

Then go for it! It may take a little time for you to get used to your new hairstyle so play with it to get the look you want.

Q: My mom says the ends of my hair don't look healthy and that she wants me to get my hair cut. How often do I need to cut my hair?

A: For your hair to be healthy, it's best to have it trimmed every six to eight weeks. If you look at the bottom of your hair carefully, you may notice strands of hair that look like they're split in two. Split ends are damaged, dead hair that won't grow, so getting them trimmed off will help your hair look and feel beautiful. If you have shorter hair, getting a trim will keep your fun style in shape. If you are growing your hair, a trim will keep your hair healthy as it grows to your desired length.

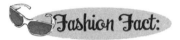

Fashion Fact:

During the 1840's, little girls usually wore their hair loose, short to shoulder length, with a part in the middle. Older girls sometimes wore their hair in ringlets around their ears or pulled back in a knot.

What Does the Bible Say?

And even the very hairs of your head are all numbered. So don't be afraid; you are worth more than many sparrows.

~ *Matthew 10:30-31*

I waited patiently for the LORD; he turned to me and heard my cry.

~ *Psalm 40:1*

A patient man has great understanding, but a quick-tempered man displays folly.

~ *Proverbs 14:29*

Be joyful in hope, patient in affliction, faithful in prayer.

~ *Romans 12:12*

✉ Letters to God

Hi God, So, I talked with Caleb today at recess. He told me again how sorry he was for spitting his gum in my hair. Then, he told me he liked my new haircut. At first, I didn't know if he was just saying that or if he really meant it, but then he looked me right in the eye and smiled.

I smiled back. I don't want there to be any weirdness between us, so I said, "I forgive you," and put out my hand so we could shake on it. All is forgiven and forgotten.

I think our math teacher felt bad that I had to have my hair cut off because he made a sign that says, "Absolutely NO GUM in class."

I've been having fun fixing my hair before school. This short hair thing is not so bad; in fact, it takes less time to wash, dry, and brush, and I can still wear my cute clips and headbands.

I still want my long hair back, but my mom told me it will grow back eventually.

Please, God, give me lots of patience!

Love, —Leah

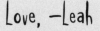

Now, it's your turn. Write your own letter to God and tell Him about a time you had to be patient for something.

_____

_____

_____

_____

_____

_____

_____

_____

_____

_____

_____

_____

_____

_____

_____

_____

_____

_____

_____

_____

Make It!

Sparkle Headband

As you make this craft project, think of a way you can show patience.

❄ What you need:

- ♡ Fabric headband
- ♡ Rhinestones
- ♡ Fabric glue

❄ What you do:

Adding rhinestones to a fabric headband is easy and fun. Holding the headband in one hand, dab a small amount of fabric glue in the center and add a rhinestone. Continue adding rhinestones until you have the look you want.

Memory Verse:

Write down the memory verse from the beginning of the chapter. Memorize it. How can you show patience to someone who offended you?

_____

_____

_____

Takeaway Thought:

Being patient with someone who's hurt you is tough. Waiting is never easy, but when you take your time before confronting someone, your words and actions will reflect Jesus.

Prayer:

Thank You, Lord, for being patient with me. Help me to be patient with others. In Jesus' name, Amen.

Chapter 4

Comfy Jeans

A new command I give you: Love one another.
As I have loved you, so you must love one another.

~John 13: 34

Claire's New Jeans

Claire tugged on the jeans, trying to make them fit. Her mom waited for her outside the dressing room.

"How's it going?" Claire heard her mom say.

"I don't know yet." Claire tried to button and zip the jeans. *It's hopeless,* Claire thought. "Not good," she said aloud.

"We should try a different store," said Mom. "Why don't you hand them to me and I'll hang them up."

Claire pulled off the jeans and handed them over the top of the dressing room. She knew her mom would be glad they didn't fit. "They hang too low at the waist," her mom had said. "Plus, they are too expensive."

Claire had begged to try them on saying, "All the girls wear them." Her mom had finally agreed, but she hadn't looked happy about it.

Claire quickly pulled on her old jeans and opened the curtain to the dressing room. "I know you're happy they didn't fit," Claire said.

"I will be honest and say that I'm not disappointed," said Mom, hanging them up.

Claire and her mom left the store with Claire walking a few feet ahead. Why couldn't she be smaller so that the jeans would fit? Why couldn't her family be rich and buy her anything she wanted?

"Why do I always have to get plain jeans? No one else has them but me," Claire said. She turned around to face her mom. "I just want to look like everyone else!"

"I know, even I get caught in that trap," said Mom.

"What do you mean?" Claire could feel her face heat with frustration.

"Why is it that we want to look like everyone else?" said Mom. "I think it's because we're afraid to look different."

Claire walked ahead. What her mom said didn't make sense. If Claire ooked in her mom's closet, she would find clothes from the dark age. Claire liked to be trendy. She liked shopping and buying the newest thing. The problem was, her parents didn't have enough money to buy her much of what she wanted.

"I want to go home," Claire called over her shoulder.

"I think that's a good idea," said Mom. "We'll try again another day."

The car ride home was awkward. Claire sat in the back seat leaning her head against the headrest with her eyes closed. She pretended to sleep so that her mom wouldn't bug her about the jeans.

After her mom hit the garage door button and pulled into the garage, she shut the engine off and turned to face her daughter. "Claire, I just wanted to tell you that I love you very much and I only want the best for you."

"The best thing would be to buy me a pair of jeans that I like," Claire responded. She opened the car door and ran into the house.

Tears streamed down Claire's cheeks as she slipped into the bathroom and locked the door. *Mom doesn't understand what it's like to be a kid,* she thought. Claire sat on the bathroom rug and leaned her head against the cabinet. Finally, she stood up, threw a wadded up tissue into the trashcan, played with her hair, and stared at herself in the mirror. She didn't know how much time had passed. She hoped her mom would knock on the bathroom door, but nothing happened. When she could take it no longer, Claire slowly opened the door and poked her head out. Then, she quietly snuck down the hall to her room and closed the door behind her.

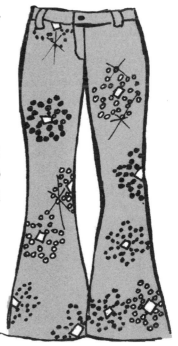

Claire sat on her bed and decided she was going to be mad at her mom until she got her some cute new jeans. She wondered how long that would be. If they went shopping tomorrow, it would be only twenty-four hours. She could stay mad for twenty-four hours.

Then, the smell of Mexican food filled Claire's nostrils. Her mouth watered. She sat up. Her stomach growled.

"Claire," called her mom. "Come set the table." Claire walked down the hall to the kitchen.

"Mom, if you really loved me you would buy me some jeans like all my friend's have," Claire blurted without thinking. *So much for keeping quiet for twenty-four hours*, she scolded herself.

"Claire, I love you because you are YOU, not because of the jeans you wear," said Mom.

Claire didn't know what to say. She wanted everyone else to like her too. She thought it was important to wear what everyone else wore, but arguing with her mom was exhausting. She knew her parents couldn't afford to buy her expensive jeans.

The thing she liked best about the jeans she saw at the store were all the rhinestones that were in the shape of flowers. *Maybe I can dress up the jeans I already have*, she thought.

"Hey Mom," said Claire. "I have an idea."

"What's that?"

"Can you help me add rhinestones to my old jeans?"

"I would love to help you," said Mom. "What a great idea."

"Thanks, Mom." Claire snatched a chip, popped it in her mouth, and grinned. "Oh, and I love you, too."

What Do You Think? ???

Do you have a favorite pair of jeans? Where did you buy them? Why do you like them?

_____

_____

_____

_____

Why did Claire decide to add rhinestones to her jeans? Do you think she showed her mom love by finding a different solution to the problem?

_____

_____

_____

_____

Do you show love to others? How?

_____

_____

_____

_____

_____

Style Tip!

✔ Finding a great pair of jeans that fit well is sometimes difficult, so when you do, consider buying a few pairs, especially if they are on sale. If your old jeans are too short, cut them into shorts!

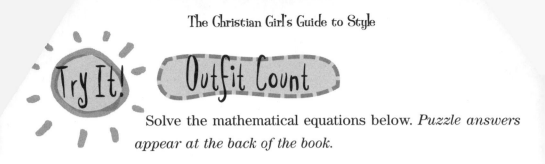

Try It! — Outfit Count

Solve the mathematical equations below. *Puzzle answers appear at the back of the book.*

Susie has a pink shirt, a purple shirt, and a turquoise shirt. She also has a pair of blue jeans and pair of white jeans. How many different outfits can she make? Write down the different combinations so that you get them all.

_____

_____

_____

_____

Suppose Susie also has a pair of black jeans. Now how many different outfits can she make?

_____

_____

_____

_____

If Susie had three shirts, three pairs of jeans and two sweaters, how many different outfits could she make?

_____

_____

_____

_____

Did you know?

Two visionary immigrants named **Levi Strauss** and **Jacob Davis** turned denim, thread, and metal rivets into the most popular clothing product in the world. **T**he first jeans were called "waist overalls." It wasn't until **1960** that the word "jeans" came about. Denim material is unique because it is woven with two yarn colors: the blue or "indigo" yarn, and the "filler" yarn, which is not dyed. **L**ook at the inside of your jeans to see the light color!

Fashion Tip: Jeans can be casual or dressy depending on what you wear them with. If you wear jeans with sneakers and a T-shirt, you're all set to go to a Saturday family picnic, but if you wear jeans with cute sandals and a pretty top, you're ready to go out on the town.

Ask Kelsey!*

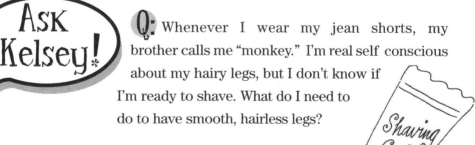

Q: Whenever I wear my jean shorts, my brother calls me "monkey." I'm real self conscious about my hairy legs, but I don't know if I'm ready to shave. What do I need to do to have smooth, hairless legs?

A: Shaving your legs (and armpits, for that matter) is a big decision because once you shave, the hair will come back coarser and thicker, so it will need to be shaved again and again. Make sure you get permission before going ahead with it. You can shop with your mom for the necessary supplies: a razor, and shaving cream. Make sure you ask your mom for help on the first shave!

Q: I see television commercials for jeans all the time. I'm so confused with all the different styles. How do I know what type of jeans I should buy?

A: Jeans come in a variety of washings, cuts, and styles. Match these with your body type for the most flattering look:

Stonewashed jeans have a lighter color and have well-worn look.

Dark jeans have a deep blue color and are dressier.

Distressed jeans have holes and look like your cat shredded them in a few places.

Low-rise jeans sit low on the waist.

Boot-cut jeans are loose on the leg and wide by the ankle, perfect for boots and winter.

Skinny jeans are tight from your hips down to your ankles.

Here are some suggestions for different body types:

If you are naturally *slim,* you would look great in jeans that run straight from your hip to your knee, with a slight flare at the ankle. If you try low-rise jeans, make sure they are high enough in the back so when you sit down you won't be embarrassed by what others may see.

If you are *curvy,* try a boot-cut jean in a dark color.

If you are *sporty,* choose a comfortable pair of traditional jeans. Whatever you choose, make sure they are comfortable because they will shrink a little in the wash.

As God's girl, you want to wear clothes that make a statement about who you are in Christ. Jeans that are too tight do not enhance your unique you.

Q: I love my jeans. My mom bought me three pairs the other day. The only problem is that my legs are so short that my jeans drag on the floor. Help!

A: Jeans that are too long can be hazardous when you're running and playing, so it's best to get them shortened. If your mom sews, she can probably alter them, or you may need a tailor to hem them. But first, have your mom wash your jeans according to the care instructions in case they shrink up a bit.

Find an old pair of jeans that you like the length of, and measure the inseam (the seam inside the pant leg). You can also have your mom pin the bottom of the jeans so that the pant's hem rests comfortably on the top of your shoes. The most important thing to do when hemming a pair of jeans is to have your mom or the tailor reattach the original hem (bottom part of the jeans) after cutting off the necessary amount. Why? Because then it will look like your jeans were never shortened.

What Does the Bible Say?

Praise the Lord. Give thanks to the LORD, for he is good; his love endures forever.

~ Psalm 106:1

For God so loved the world that He gave His one and only Son, that whoever believes in Him shall not perish but have eternal life.

~ John 3:16

Dear friends, let us love one another, for love comes from God.

~ 1 John 4:7

✉ Letters to God

Hey God! I love my old jeans—no make that my "new and improved" sparkly jeans. My mom and I added rhinestones in the shape of flowers down the right side and on the back pocket. I absolutely LOVE them!

I went to school the next Monday and my best friend ran up to me and twirled me around. She said, "Whoa, Claire, nice jeans. Where'd you get them?"

"Claire's Jean Shop," I joked.

She looked at me like I lost my marbles.

I laughed. "My mom and I decorated my old jeans."

"No way!" she said. "Do you think your mom would help me decorate an old pair of my jeans?"

My jaw dropped to my chest. Was I hearing her correctly? "What?" I asked.

She nodded. "I really don't like looking like everyone else. I want an original pair of jeans like you."

Wow. I couldn't wait to tell my mom. I smiled the rest of the day.

God, thank You for loving me and for giving me such a great mom. Help me to show her how much I love her.

—Claire

Now, it's your turn. Write your own letter to God and tell Him about a time you felt loved or showed love to someone else.

_____

_____

_____

_____

_____

_____

_____

_____

_____

_____

_____

_____

_____

_____

_____

_____

_____

_____

_____

Make It!

Beaded Jute Belt

God commands you to love others as He loved you. As you wrap this belt around you, let it remind you not only of His great love for you, but also to think about how you can show that love to others.

✳ What you will need:
- ♡ An old belt
- ♡ Jute
- ♡ Beads
- ♡ Scissors or hole punch

✳ What you do:

Cut off the buckle and the holes on each end of the belt. With adult supervision, make two round holes one inch from each end of the belt with a hole punch or the point of a scissors. The jute will cover any rough edges.

Cut two pieces of jute 18" long and fold each piece in half. Push the fold through the belt hole to make a loop, and then put the ends through the loop. Pull tight.

Add fun beads to the jute—as many as you like. Tie in a knot or bow and let the beaded jute hang down.

Memory Verse:

Write down the memory verse from the beginning of the chapter.
Memorize it. Consider how you can show love to others.

_____

_____

_____

Takeaway Thought:

Do you know how far the heavens are above the earth? That's how much
God loves you! By loving God the most, you will be able to love others.

Prayer:

Thank You, Lord that Your love endures forever. Help me to love others.
In Jesus' name, Amen.

Chapter 5

Skirts

Let your gentleness be evident to all. The Lord is near.

~Philippians 4:5

Eve's Matching Skirt

Eve walked into her Sunday school class and sat down next to her friend Mary.

"Oh no, can you believe it?" said Mary loudly. "We're wearing the same skirt!"

Eve looked down at her friend's skirt and shook her head. No, she couldn't believe it. In fact, Mary was with Eve and her mom a month ago when Mom bought the skirt for Eve's birthday.

Eve bit her lower lip as she stared at the twin skirt her friend was wearing.

"I guess we'll have to call each other when we want to wear it, so this won't happen again," Mary said.

"Okay class, let's settle down," said the Sunday school teacher. "Let's get going on today's lesson."

The class passed by in a blur. Eve didn't listen to one word the teacher said. She was too distracted and hurt. Eve thought about all the things that she and Mary had bought together—a funny T-shirt, a purse, even a headband. Why would Mary buy the same skirt?

Before she realized it, the teacher had dismissed the kids to meet their parents for church. Eve stood and turned around. Mary was showing off her skirt to a group of girls, making a big deal of the turquoise and green flowered pattern and how it swished when she twirled. *I did that when I was three*, thought Eve. Anger started to build as she watched Mary walk off with the group.

Eve sprinted toward the sanctuary to meet her parents. She found them in their usual seats—ten rows from the front. She raced down the aisle and plopped down next to them. "Mom, can we go home?" she asked.

"What's wrong?" asked her mom.

"Can we just go home?" Eve asked again, grabbing handfuls of skirt material in each hand.

"You need to tell me what's going on," said Mom. "The service is about to start."

"Never mind," Eve sighed, leaning her head on her hand. "Can we just go home right after church is over? Please? Let's not stop to talk to anyone on the way out."

"Okay," said Mom, "but after we leave we need to talk about what's bothering you."

"Fine," Eve said, slouching down in the pew.

The musicians started playing worship songs. Eve knew Mary usually sat with her dad a few rows back. She didn't even want to turn around and look.

The church service dragged on. Eve felt her insides churning. Instead of listening to the sermon, she thought of all kinds of mean things to say to Mary. Maybe she would tell her what was on her mind after the service was over—maybe even in front of their friends. Wouldn't that make Mary embarrassed? Eve formulated a plan as the service went on.

She looked at her parents as they sang the last song. Their eyes were closed and their chins were slightly tilted upwards like they were singing right to Jesus. Eve didn't feel like singing. Even if she wanted to, she didn't think the words would come out. The thoughts she was having toward her friend stopped her from worshiping God.

"Eve, honey, let's go," said Mom when the service was over.

Eve grabbed her bulletin from the pew. As they headed up the aisle, E spotted Mary standing by the door giving her a funny look.

"There's your friend Mary," said Mom. "And look, you're wearing the same skirt."

"Thanks for reminding me," said Eve as they approached her friend.

"Eve, can I talk to you a minute?" asked Mary.

"I guess so," Eve said. She looked at her parents. "I'll be just a minute." Her parents turned and started talking with some friends.

"Why didn't you get mad at me?" asked Mary. "I thought you would."

"Who says I'm not mad?" Eve said. She folded her arms and furrowed her eyebrows.

"Because you didn't say anything when I told you we were wearing the same skirt," said Mary.

"That's because I didn't know what to say," said Eve. "I thought of all kinds of mean things to say to you during the sermon, but then I didn't want to say them. I guess I only have one question: Why?"

Mary looked down and sighed. "This skirt reminds me of the day we went shopping. It was such a fun day with you and your mom. It's hard having divorced parents. I don't get to see my mom very often."

Eve shook her head in acknowledgement. She knew Mary was having a hard time lately and really missed her mom. "You know what," said Eve, "you don't need to call me when you're going to wear your skirt. We can just be twins!"

"Really?" asked Mary.

"Really." Eve linked arms with her best friend. "Don't you just love the way this skirt swishes when you twirl?"

What Do You Think? ??

Do you have a favorite dress or skirt? What does it look like?

_____

_____

_____

How did Eve respond when she discovered her friend's real reason for buying the same skirt?

_____

_____

_____

Are you able to speak with gentle words when you're upset?

_____

_____

_____

Style Tip!

Mini skirts are fun to wear, but how short is too short? Look in the mirror. Try sitting. Can you see anything you wouldn't want others to see? Bend over. Does it ride up to embarrassing heights? If you said, "yes" to either question, your mini skirt is too short. If you just can't seem to part with it, sew the bottom closed and turn it into a book bag.

Did you know?

You are royalty. God sees you as a princess—holy and blameless in his sight. Read Ephesians 1: 3-14 for more on this! It's important to realize how God sees you so that when you look at yourself in the mirror, you'll view yourself the same way God sees you.

Fashion Tip: When you're wearing a fancy dress or skirt, don't forget good posture—stand up straight, shoulders back, and hold your head up high.

Ask Kelsey!

Q: I love to wear skirts because they're so comfortable, but I've noticed only a few girls in my class wear them. Why?

A: Some girls are more active and prefer to wear pants or jeans, while other girls enjoy the more feminine look of a skirt. The bottom line is this: if you love to wear skirts, wear them! It's all part of being the unique you!

Q: I'm going to a daddy-daughter dance and I don't know what kind of a dress to wear. Any ideas?

A: This is your night to look and feel your best! If you don't own a nice dress, now is the time to go shopping. Dresses are sewn in a number of different fabrics. Some fancier dresses are made of satin, silk, taffeta, or velvet and decorated with lace, pearls, sequins, embroidery, and/or ruffles. Other simpler dresses and skirts are made of cotton.

For the daddy-daughter dance, it's best to find out how formal the event is going to be, and shop with your style in mind. No matter what dress you buy, if you go to the dance with a gentle spirit, your inner beauty will shine through and you'll look amazing!

Q: My mom makes me wear a dress or a skirt to church. Why?

A: Wearing a dress or skirt to church shows that you want to look your best for God. Not all church members wear dressier clothing. In fact, people at some churches wear jeans and tees. The most important thing you can do right now is listen to your parents. Jump into that skirt with a smile on your face. You'll look simply beautiful, and God will appreciate that you are dressing up for Him.

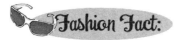 **Fashion Fact:**

In the 1890's girls wore white frilly dresses, often covered with lace and ribbons. Their skirts ended just below the knee on young girls and just above the ankle for teenagers. Girls wore aprons or pinafores over their dresses to keep them nice and clean.

What Does the Bible Say?

Rejoice greatly, O Daughter of Zion! Shout, Daughter of Jerusalem! See, your king comes to you, righteous and having salvation, gentle and riding on a donkey, on a colt, the foal of a donkey.

~ Zechariah 9:9

Take my yoke upon you and learn from me, for I am gentle and humble in heart, and you will find rest for your souls.

~ Matthew 11:29

But in your hearts set apart Christ as Lord. Always be prepared to give an answer to everyone who asks you to give the reason for the hope that you have. But do this with gentleness and respect.

~ 1 Peter 3:15

✉ Letters to God

Hey there, God! It's funny how things turn out. I was fuming mad when I saw that Mary had bought the same skirt as me. I didn't even know what the sermon was about at church. When I realized the reason Mary bought the skirt, it made me feel totally different. I'm sure glad I didn't blow up in front of the whole congregation!

After church I asked Mary if she could come over to my house. Her dad said it was okay because he wanted to watch the football game on T.V. this afternoon.

Mary and I hung out in my bedroom. We listened to our favorite CD and danced and twirled in our matching skirts. We laughed so hard.

Oh, by the way, Mary said she was sorry for hurting my feelings and bragging in front of the other girls in Sunday school. She told me she should have called me first and asked if she could buy the same skirt. It sure would have saved me from thinking all those crazy mean thoughts during church!

I did figure out a couple of things today. I'm glad that Mary is my best friend with or without a matching skirt. And, it's best to talk in a calm and gentle way.

Bye for now—Eve

Now, it's your turn. Write your own letter to God and tell Him about a time you responded with gentle words.

Make It!

Pillowcase Skirt

Being gentle in your words and actions will
draw others to you. As you make this skirt, think
about how you can respond in a gentle way to
those around you.

❋ What you need:

- ♡ Pillowcase
- ♡ Measuring tape
- ♡ Scissors
- ♡ Washable fabric glue
- ♡ Clear nail polish
- ♡ Safety pin
- ♡ 45-inch cotton drawstring

❋ What you do:

Step 1: Lay the pillowcase flat and carefully cut off the closed end. Step
inside the pillowcase with the cut end at your waist. Decide how long you
want your skirt to be, and measure from the hem (what will be the
bottom of the skirt) to your waist. Step out of the pillowcase. Measuring
once again, add 1½ inches to desired length. Cut any excess material
from the cut edge.

Step 2: Turn the pillowcase inside out. With a parent's help, iron down ½ inch along the cut edge all the way around. Then, iron down an additional inch.

Step 3: Apply fabric glue with a small brush between the two ironed folds to form a waistband. Let it dry.

Step 4: Take some clear nail polish and apply a single line of polish at the center of the waistband. Let it dry. Apply a second coat of nail polish. After the second coat is dry, take your scissors and cut a slit in the middle of the nail polish for the drawstring.

Step 5: Attach a safety pin to one end of the drawstring and feed it through the waistband. Remove the safety pin and tie knots to each end of the drawstring. Your pillowcase skirt is ready to wear!

 **Memory Verse:**

Write down the memory verse from the beginning of the chapter. Memorize it and practice gentleness today.

_____

_____

_____

_____

 **Takeaway Thought:**

When you think about it, being gentle not only shows respect but also turns away anger. Because God is gentle, you can find rest in Him.

Prayer:

Thank You, Lord that You are gentle and humble in heart. Help me to be gentle in my words and actions. In Jesus' name, Amen.

Chapter 6

Hats

Be completely humble and gentle; be patient,
bearing with one another in love.

~ Ephesians 4: 2

Anna Gets A Hit

"Strike one," said the umpire as he turned his body sideways and pumped his fist in the air.

Anna straightened her helmet and pushed her hair away from her face with her left hand. She looked around the infield and noted the players standing on first and second base. A knot formed in her stomach. They needed three more runs to win the game. There were two outs already—one more and the game would be over.

"Get a hit, Anna," called her coach standing near first base.

Anna swung her bat a few times to show the pitcher where to throw the ball. The next pitch was thrown too high and Anna didn't flinch.

"Ball one," said the umpire.

Anna loved to play softball. This was her third year with the all-girl softball team. She was known for hitting the ball and usually got a base hit.

The next pitch was thrown. Perfect.

Come on, hit the ball, Anna thought. She swung. And missed.

"Strike two," said the umpire once again pumping his fist in the air.

Does he have to do that? Anna thought. She tapped her shoes with the end of the bat and once again settled into position. Butterflies flitted around her stomach.

The pitch was thrown. As the ball headed towards home plate, Anna lifted her back elbow, her eyes glued on the ball; and then, CRACK! A hit. Anna watched the ball fly over the shortstop's head.

"Run," yelled Anna's coach as he motioned her down the line.

Anna moved her legs as fast as they would go. Her helmet flew off her head as she sprinted toward first base. The ball dropped between two outfielders and the bases were loaded. The ball was quickly thrown to the pitcher and the third base coach signaled the runners to hold-up.

The parents of the Powder Puffs were on their feet, clapping wildly.

"Go, Powder Puffs," called Anna's mom through a small pink megaphone. Anna gave her mom a thumbs-up.

Anna saw Mara put on a hard helmet and grab a bat. *Oh, no, not Mara. She never gets a hit.*

Mara headed towards home plate.

We're doomed! Anna thought. She wanted to cover her face with her baseball cap. They all might as well go home. There was no way Mara was going to hit the ball. Anna couldn't even think of a time Mara had hit the ball in practice.

"Let's go, Mara," called the coach. "Keep your eye on the ball."

Strikes one and two came in quick succession. Balls one, two, and three came next and it was a full count. Anna knew the best her team could hope for was ball four so Mara could walk to first base, which would add a run for the Powder Puffs.

The pitcher threw the ball. "Strike three, you're out!" announced the umpire, pumping his fist in the air.

"NO!" Anna yelled. She stomped her foot in protest. "I can't believe i_ We lost! We were so close!"

The coach called the girls together to form a circle. "Two, four, six, eight, who do we appreciate, Banana Slugs, Banana Slugs, Banana Slugs!" the Powder Puffs shouted.

Anna muttered the cheer. *Why would the coach put Mara up to bat knowing she would strike out and lose the game?*

"Okay, girls, let's go shake their hands," said the coach.

Mara stood in front of Anna as they gave the other team high fives. "Good game," they said up and down the line.

"Hey, Anna," said Mara. "I'm sorry we lost."

"I bet you are. Next time, try swinging the bat," Anna huffed. She marched off to find her parents.

"That was a great game," Anna's mom said.

"It was a great game until the coach put Mara up to bat," Anna replied. She took off her baseball cap and wiped her forehead with the back of her hand.

"Don't be too hard on Mara," said Dad. "She's probably being hard enough on herself."

"Yeah, but she lost the game," Anna sighed as she opened the car door and plopped in her seat.

"That could have been you," said Dad. "It's a lot of pressure when there are two outs."

"But did you see the hit I made?" said Anna. "It flew way over the shortstop's head."

"It was a good hit," said Mom. "Come on, let's go home."

Once home, Anna stripped out of her clothes and hopped in the shower. As the water poured down, she replayed the game in her head. Maybe she had been too hard on Mara. After all, Mara was a good catcher. She did stop the other team from scoring two runs.

Anna dried herself off and slipped into her robe. She walked to her bedroom, and picked up her baseball hat. "Hey, wait a minute," Anna said out loud. The cap looked different. She looked inside the cap and saw the name *Mara* written in permanent marker. *Oh, no!* Anna tried to thin back to the game and figure out how she grabbed Mara's hat. Nothing came to mind.

"Hey Mom," called Anna. "Can I use the phone?"

"Sure," said Mom, "but we're going out to dinner in half an hour."

Anna thought back to the comment she made to Mara after the teams shook hands. A knot formed in her stomach as she dialed Mara's number.

Mara answered the phone.

"You'll never believe this, but somehow I grabbed your baseball hat," said Anna.

"I have yours, too," said Mara. There was a moment of silence.

Anna bit her lower lip and ran her fingers through her wet hair. "I'm sorry for what I said to you at the game," she said.

"That's okay," Mara sighed. "Sorry I lost the game."

"But you didn't lose the game. In fact, you tagged a couple out at home plate, remember?" said Anna.

"Yeah, but I froze at bat," said Mara.

"Do you want to come over tomorrow?" said Anna. "I'll help you with your swing."

"Really?" said Mara. "You'd do that for me?"

"For us!" said Anna. "We're a team!"

What Do You Think? ???

Do you have a favorite hat? What does it look like?

_____

_____

_____

_____

What did Anna discover after reflecting on the loss of the softball game? Was it one person's fault?

_____

_____

_____

_____

What three things do we need in order to bear with one another in love according to Ephesians 4:2?

_____

_____

_____

_____

_____

_____

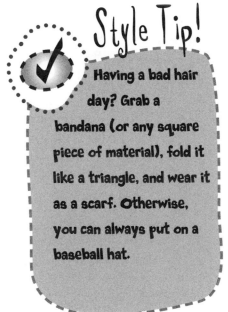

Style Tip!

Having a bad hair day? Grab a bandana (or any square piece of material), fold it like a triangle, and wear it as a scarf. Otherwise, you can always put on a baseball hat.

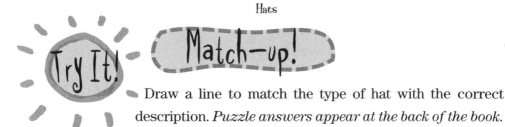

Try It! Match-up!

Draw a line to match the type of hat with the correct description. *Puzzle answers appear at the back of the book.*

Baseball cap	a hat, usually felt, with a high crown and a wide brim
Beanie	a covering of fine fabric or net for the face and head, worn by a bride
Beret	a knitted cap usually worn in cold weather
Bonnet	a hat framing the face and usually tied under the chin
Bowler	a flat round soft hat, usually woolen, with a tight fitting headband
Cowgirl hat	oval hat with a round, rigid crown and a small, shaped, curved brim, also known as a derby
Helmet	a Mexican coned hat with a very wide brim, usually made of straw
Sombrero	a close-fitting cap with a visor
Veil	a partial brim without a crown, used as a shade to protect from sun
Visor	a hat made of hard material and worn to protect the head

Did you know?

There are many reasons to wear a hat: sun protection, as part of a uniform, to keep your head clean, to keep your head warm, to complete an outfit, or to hide a bad hair day! Hats can be soft or structured, dressy or casual.

Fashion Tip: Store your nicer hats and caps in hat boxes to keep them clean and dust free. Your baseball hats and everyday caps can be stored on coat racks, in plastic bags or on bookshelves.

Ask Kelsey!

Q: I love hats, but I don't think they look good on me. What style of hat should I wear?

A: If you love hats, wear them! Hats are fun and come in a variety of shapes, colors, and textures. The important thing is to wear a hat that you feel comfortable and confident in, and to choose a style that fits the occasion. Since hats are worn so close to your face, it is important for the hat to fit the size of your face and flatter your skin tone. If you have paler skin, a warmer color such as pink is a good choice. If you have darker skin, you can wear many different colors, but you should definitely avoid black. If you have a small face, it's best to wear a hat with a smaller crown (top part of the hat) and brim (projecting edge); and if you have a larger face, wear a bigger crown and brim. The key is to play up your best features and to wear the hat you love!

Q: My mom tells me to wear a hat whenever I go in the sun. Why?

A: The sun's rays are the strongest in the middle of the day between 11:00 a.m. and 3:00 p.m. If you can't avoid the sun during this time, then you should cover up with a hat that has a brim to protect your face and the back of your neck from those ultraviolet rays. A straw sun hat is an excellent choice and looks great, too.

Q: My friend's family invited me to go skiing with them. My dad packed me a ski hat along with ski gloves and a scarf. I don't want to wear the hat because it will mess up my hair. Help!

A: 70% of heat lost is through your head, hands, and feet, so you don't want to give any of it away if you don't have to. That means— wear the hat! And make sure your ears are covered. Knitted beanie hats come in an assortment of cute colors and designs. You can even match the color of your hat to your jacket, scarf, and gloves.

And remember—every skier has hat hair! One of the fun things about skiing is that you get to bundle up. The higher you go up the mountain on a chair lift, the colder it may be, so you want to be prepared from your head down to your toes.

Fashion Fact:

During the Civil War era in the 1860's, girls wore bonnets when they went outside. Fabric sunbonnets were the most popular since they were sturdy and could be washed. Straw hats were worn in hot weather.

What Does the Bible Say?

But you are a shield around me, O LORD; you bestow glory on me and lift up my head.

~ Psalm 3:3

Carry each other's burdens, and in this way you will fulfill the law of Christ.

~ Galatians 6:2

Bear with each other and forgive whatever grievances you may have against one another. Forgive as the Lord forgave you.

~ Colossians 3:13

However, if you suffer as a Christian, do not be ashamed, but praise God that you bear that name.

~ 1 Peter 4:16

Letters to God

Hey God, My stomach is full from the pizza I just ate from Antonelli's. Yum. I ate three slices of my favorite kind, ham and pineapple. Then, my parents took me to get ice cream for playing my best softball game yet.

You'll never guess who I saw at the ice cream shop . . . you guessed it: Mara, along with her two sisters and her parents. I'm sure glad I apologized when we talked on the phone. I would've felt real bad for the way I treated her at the ball field. I don't know what I was thinking. I guess I wanted to win more than I wanted to be nice to my teammate.

I walked up to Mara with my double chocolate crunch ice cream cone and said, "Hi Mara."

Mara took her vanilla ice cream cone from the worker.

"You're still coming tomorrow, right?" I asked. I bit my cone at the tip and caught the drops of ice cream coming out of the bottom.

"Yep," Mara answered. "Maybe I'll get a hit next time."

"Doesn't matter, just do your best," I said, stuffing the rest of the cone in my mouth. Mara smiled.

God, help me to be more humble, gentle, and patient, especially tomorrow when Mara practices her batting!

Love, —Anna

now, it's your turn. Write your own letter to God and tell Him about a time you had to bear with someone in love.

_____

_____

_____

_____

_____

_____

_____

_____

_____

_____

_____

_____

_____

_____

_____

_____

_____

_____

_____

_____

Decoupage Painter's Cap

As you make this project, remember to be humble and gentle with others!

✳ What you need:

♡ Painter's cap
♡ Pictures
♡ White glue
♡ Popsicle stick
♡ Cotton swab
♡ Damp rag
♡ Fabric paint
♡ Paintbrush

✳ What you do:

Step 1: Paint your painter's cap with fabric paint. This will seal the cap. Let it dry. Cut out your pictures. The pictures can be cut out of magazines, catalogs, books, wrapping paper, wallpaper, greeting cards, fabric, etc. You can also buy designed paper made especially for decoupage.

Step 2: Arrange the pictures before you add the glue. The pictures can be in any design and can also overlap.

Step 3: Completely coat the back of the pictures with your glue, spreading it with a cotton swab. You should also put a thin layer of glue on the hat in the area where you are sticking the pictures.

Step 4: Stick the pictures on the hat. Use your finger to gently push down the pictures and push out any wrinkles with the popsicle stick. Use a damp rag to wipe away any excess glue.

Step 5: Now, coat your cap completely with diluted white glue (approximately 3 parts glue to 1 part water). Let this dry completely. You can continue to add coats of glue until you get the desired results. You will, however, want to keep adding coats until the edges of the pictures are smooth. Let dry.

* **Optional:** Add sequins and rhinestones for a sparkly look!

Memory Verse:

Write down the memory verse from the beginning of the chapter. Memorize it. How can you bear with others in love?

_____

_____

_____

 Takeaway Thought:

Bearing with others shows that you are a team player who is humble, gentle, and patient. Knowing that God daily bears your burdens will help you bear with others.

Prayer:

Thank You, Lord, for bearing my burdens. Help me to be a team player and bear with others in love. In Jesus' name, Amen.

Chapter 7

Beautiful Nails

If we confess our sins, he is faithful and just and will forgive our sins and purify us from all unrighteousness.

~ 1 John 1:9

Joy Tells a Lie

Joy snuck into her parents' bathroom. She tiptoed to the sink, opened the top drawer of the vanity, and rummaged through her mother's things. "Now where is that nail polish?" Joy muttered. Ever since she had seen her mom wear the pretty pink color, Joy had wanted to see how it would look on her own nails. After she pushed aside the hairbrush, toothpaste, and face cream, she discovered the hot pink nail polish.

Ah, there it is!

She snatched the small bottle, quickly shut the drawer, and headed out of the bathroom through her parents' bedroom.

Her mom walked in with a basket of clean laundry. "What were you doing in there?" she asked.

"Oh, hi, Mom," Joy said. She quickly put her hands in her jean pockets hoping to disguise the nail polish. "I, um, was trying to find something."

"What were you trying to find in *my* bathroom?" Mom emptied the contents of the laundry basket onto the bed.

"Oh, just trying to find a hairbrush," lied Joy. "You know how they seem to disappear."

"Try looking in your backpack," Mom said. She picked up the empty laundry basket in one hand, the other on her hip. "You usually keep one in there."

"Okay." Joy sidestepped toward the door, hoping to make it to her bedroom so she could try the nail polish.

"Do you have any laundry you need washed?" asked Mom.

"Uh, I think so."

"Fill up this basket with dirty clothes and bring it to the laundry room, please. I'll wash them this afternoon." Mom handed the laundry basket to Joy.

Joy reached for the laundry basket with her left hand, keeping her right hand tucked in her pocket firmly clutching the nail polish. She walked backwards to the door, turned around, and sprinted to her room, where she closed the door behind her.

Joy set the laundry basket on the floor, and then sat at her desk. She hoisted her left foot up, opened the "Flamingo" colored nail polish, and painted each toenail.

Once her left foot was done, Joy swung her right foot up...and accidentally knocked over the nail polish "Oops!" She watched the nail polish trickle onto her desk.

Hopping on her right foot, Joy hurried out of her room to the main bathroom and grabbed a few squares of toilet paper. She hobbled back to her bedroom and noticed some nail polish on the carpet. *Oh, no!* Joy quickly wiped the nail polish off of her desk, and then ran back to the bathroom to get a wet washcloth.

Joy sat on the floor and attempted to clean the carpet. She saw that the painted toes on her left foot were now smeared, and nail polish had gotten on the hem of her jeans. She slipped the jeans off and placed them in the laundry basket, then grabbed a pair of sweatpants and put them on.

Joy decided the nail polish wasn't worth any more effort, so she took the small bottle, tiptoed back to her mother's bathroom, and slipped the polish into the top drawer.

"Joy," called Mom, "where's your laundry?"

"It's coming," said Joy, running back to her room. She filled the laundry basket with her dirty clothes, and carried it downstairs.

"Thanks," said Mom.

Joy watched her mom reach down to put the laundry in the washer. Her mom stopped when she noticed Joy's toes. "Joy," said Mom, "why are some of your nails painted with my polish?"

In the rush, Joy had forgotten about her toes. "Oops. I'm in trouble, huh?"

"Is that why you were in my bathroom?" asked Mom.

"Yes." Joy tried to cover her toes with her right foot. "I'm sorry. I really made a mess of things, didn't I?"

"For starters, you lied to me," said Mom.

"I know," said Joy.

"And you took my favorite nail polish without asking."

Joy frowned.

"Is there anything else you want to say?" asked Mom.

"I also spilled it on my desk, my carpet, and my favorite jeans." Joy knew it was best to confess it all.

"Oh Joy," said Mom. "What am I going to do with you?"

"Forgive and forget?" Joy grinned.

"Come here." Mom opened her arms wide. "Just don't do it again."

"Okay, Mom." Joy entered her mom's embrace.

"And, by the way." Mom added. "You're grounded."

"I thought so," sighed Joy.

What Do You Think? ???

Do you have a favorite nail polish? What color is it?

_____

_____

_____

What was Joy's first mistake in this story? How does one sin lead to another?

_____

_____

_____

_____

_____

_____

_____

Are you able to forgive and forget when someone wrongs you?

_____

_____

_____

_____

_____

_____

Style Tip!

✔ Is your nail polish chipping? That means it's time to use some nail polish remover and take it all off. To make your nail polish last longer, add a clear coat after painting your nails and wait at least 2 hours before doing anything with your hands. Why not polish your nails before going to bed? Just make sure they have at least 30 minutes to dry.

My Nails

Trace your hand in the space below. Create fun and original nails, coloring them any way you choose.

Did you know?

Fingernails grow about 0.02 inches a week. They grow more during the day, in the summer, and in warm and sunny climates. The fingernails on your longest fingers grow the fastest, and the more you use your hand, the faster the nails will grow because of a better blood supply.

Fashion Tip: Have you ever seen fake nails at the drugstore? They may look fun, but the sticky glue you use to attach them to your fingernails isn't good for your nails. Instead, buy a new fun new color and paint away!

Ask Kelsey!*

Q: I have a habit of biting my nails whenever I'm watching T.V., or when I'm bored or nervous. I want to stop but don't know how. Help!

A: Healthy nails are important. They protect your fingertips and make it easier to pick up tiny objects. Longer nails are especially nice when you have an itch that needs scratching. Germs tend to hide under your fingernails, so when you nibble on them, those germs go directly into your mouth. Gross.

You're not the only one who bites her nails; in fact, many people do. It's a hard habit to break, but it's worth trying. Here are a few ideas to help you stop biting and keep your nails at a healthy length.

❁ Paint your nails with a nail-biting polish your mom can buy at the store. It tastes disgusting and bitter, and will keep your fingers away from your mouth.

❁ Try spending a few minutes every day caring for your nails. Put some nice-smelling lotion on your hands, and check your nail growth regularly. Why don't you keep an emery board (fingernail file) handy so when you're tempted to chew, you can file instead?

❁ Keep your hands busy doing something else—like drawing, writing, knitting, or squeezing a soft ball.

❁ Keep your nails painted—the brighter the color the better! You won't want to ruin your new manicure!

Q: My sister washes her hands all the time. It drives me crazy. I know it's important to wash your hands before you eat and after you use the bathroom, but do I need to wash my hands constantly?

A: Since washing your hands is the best way to stop germs from spreading, yes, it's best to wash your hands throughout the day. Why? Think about the things you touch—the toilet, the telephone, door handles, a tissue, the family pet, or dust and dirt from outside. Your hands come in contact with germs all the time.

So, when should you wash your hands?

❁ Whenever your hands feel sweaty, dirty, or grimy

❁ Before touching food

❁ After using the bathroom

❁ After blowing your nose or coughing

❁ After petting an animal

❁ After playing outside

❁ Before and after visiting someone sick

You can always keep a hand sanitizer or wipes in your purse o backpack for those times when you can't get to soap and water. You'll be one clean girl!

 **Fashion Fact:**

In the 1960's, nail polish followed the lipstick trend and pastel pearl colors were in style.

 **What Does the Bible Say?**

Make it your ambition to lead a quiet life, to mind your own business and to work with your hands, just as we told you.
~ 1 Thessalonians 4:11

Help us, O God our Savior, for the glory of your name; deliver us and forgive our sins for your name's sake.
~ Psalm 79:9

Do not judge, and you will not be judged. Do not condemn, and you will not be condemned. Forgive, and you will be forgiven.
~ Luke 6:37

For I will forgive their wickedness and will remember their sins no more.
~ 1 Thessalonians 4:11

✉ Letters to God

Hi God, Okay, I'm never going to do that again! What was I thinking taking my mom's nail polish without asking? Now I'm grounded for a whole week. That reminds me . . . this afternoon I heard my mom tell her best friend the whole story on the phone. I was mad because who wants to hear their mom repeat their worst moment? So, I blew up at her and stomped off to my room.

After awhile, my mom knocked on my door. She sat next to me on my bed, played with my hair, and said she was sorry. I gave her a funny look. Then I looked down at my toes...one foot smeared with flamingo nail polish, the other normal. I started laughing. If my mom can be so forgiving, than why can't I? We hugged and I said, "I forgive you."

My mom is teaching me how to do the laundry. I have to fill the baskets with dirty laundry, put it in the washer, transfer the clean laundry to the dryer, fold it, and then put the clean clothes away. Good thing my older brother is at college. I'd hate to have to touch his dirty underwear. Yuck!

My mom also said she's going to let me buy my own nail polish with my allowance money. She said that I could even buy flamingo pink. Though now that I've tried it on, I might choose a different color instead. Maybe red! Then, Mom said that if I am responsible with my nail polish, she might even take me to get a manicure at a real nail salon place. Wouldn't that be cool?

Love, —Joy

Now, it's your turn. Write your own letter to God and tell Him about a time you forgave someone.

_____

_____

_____

_____

_____

_____

_____

_____

_____

_____

_____

_____

_____

_____

_____

_____

_____

_____

_____

Make It!

Confetti Nails

As you paint each nail, thank God for forgiving you from your sins.

What you need:

- ♡ Emery board
- ♡ Cuticle stick
- ♡ Nail polish
- ♡ Confetti
- ♡ Hand cream/lotion
- ♡ Cotton balls or cotton swabs

What you do:

After washing your hands, moisturize with a hand cream or lotion. Then, soak your fingers in a bowl of warm water to soak and soften the cuticles (the U-shaped part around your nail). Next, gently push back the cuticles using a cuticle stick or a cotton swab. Do not cut them.

Shape the nails using a double-sided emery board. Make sure you file in only one direction to avoid rough edges.

Remove any old polish by using a polish remover and cotton balls or a cotton swab dipped in remover. Be sure to remove all traces of polish.

Apply a thin coat of clear polish. This will help protect the nails and make the polish last longer. Let the polish dry.

Next, choose your polish color. Using a small amount of polish, paint each nail in three strokes beginning with the middle of the nail, then on ither side from the bottom of the nail going upward. Place a piece of confetti onto each wet nail. Complete each nail until both hands are done. Let the polish dry.

Finally, apply another coat of clear polish. Let the polish dry. Be careful for the next 30 minutes to allow all layers of nail polish to set. You're good to go. Beautiful!

Optional: Instead of choosing a colored polish, use a clear coat for a fun confetti look.

Memory Verse:

Write down the memory verse from the beginning of the chapter. Memorize it. Think of someone you need to forgive today.

_____

_____

_____

Takeaway Thought:

Just like nail polish remover, God wipes away your sins and remembers them no more. Talk to Him today, and then forgive someone else who needs your forgiveness.

Prayer:

Thank You, Lord, that You forgive. Help me to forgive others. In Jesus' name, Amen.

Chapter 8

It's All in the Tee

So then, just as you received Christ Jesus as Lord, continue to live in him, rooted and built up in Him, strengthened in the faith as you were taught, and overflowing with thankfulness.

~Colossians 2:6–7

Craft Corner

"Girls, come into the Craft Corner and we'll get started with today's craft," said Peaches, the camp counselor.

Ten chatty girls meandered over to the table where T-shirts were stacked in rows.

"Pick your size and then we'll get started with our project," said Peaches.

The girls picked through the T-shirts, making a mess of the neat piles.

Faith and Hope flew in through the door.

"There you are," Theresa said, motioning the girls over. "Where were you?"

"Hope fell down and scraped her knee, so we had to go to the nurse's station," said Faith.

"You didn't have to go with me if you didn't want to, Sis" said Hope.

"Well, you'd better pick your T-shirts before they're all gone," said Theresa.

Faith and Hope looked at the remaining T-shirts—two small, and one medium. Hope grabbed the medium before Faith had a chance.

"You know I'm bigger than you," said Faith.

"But a medium would fit me better," Hope said, holding up the T-shirt.

"But a small definitely won't fit me," Faith said.

"Now girls, bring your T-shirts to this table," said Peaches. "We're going to make tie-dyed shirts today. Make sure you put your name on the inside of your shirt before you start."

The counselor handed out permanent markers. "Now I want you to twist your T-shirts and place rubber bands every two to three inches. Or you can be creative and add more rubber bands if you'd like. Next, we'll dip the shirts in dye and then hang them up to dry."

"Come on, they're starting already," said Theresa.

It's All in the Tee

Faith grabbed the small T-shirt. *I wish Hope wasn't so stubborn!* she thought. *And after I helped her to the nurse's station.*

Faith noticed Hope carefully pinching off small sections of her T-shirt and tying them snugly with the rubber bands. Faith, on the other hand, twisted the whole T-shirt three times and casually added a few rubber bands.

"Cool, they have different colors," Theresa said, dipping her tied T-shirt in the green bucket.

"Keep your T-shirt in the dye for at least 5 minutes," Peaches said.

"There is yellow, green, and orange," said Hope.

"No purple?" Faith asked. She dropped her T-shirt into the bucket with the yellow dye.

Hope picked orange.

"Okay girls, your five minutes are up," said Peaches. "Make sure you wear these rubber gloves when you get your T-shirts out of the dye, and take off the rubber bands."

"Wow, these look kind of cool," Faith said, looking at all the shirts hanging out to dry.

"Look at the way every design looks different," said Theresa.

"I think I like Hope's T-shirt best of all," said Faith.

"After you help clean up, you may go to the snack shack, and then to the pool," instructed Peaches.

"I think I'll skip swimming. My knee hurts." Hope collected the extra rubber bands.

Theresa grabbed one side of the bucket containing the green dye. "My hair turns green every summer I go to camp." Theresa laughed. "My mom thinks I live in the water."

"Well, you are a fish," said Faith grabbing the other side. "I'll swim with you. Hey, Hope, will you be okay?"

"Yeah," Hope said. She handed the rubber bands to the counselor and hobbled off to her cabin.

"Do you think our T-shirts are dry?" Theresa said, hopping out of the pool. She wrapped herself in a towel and slipped into her flip-flops.

"We'll check after we change," Faith said. She led the way to their cabin.

"Surprise!" said Hope to the girls as they entered.

"What's going on?" Faith asked. She looked over at Theresa. Theresa shrugged her shoulders.

"What are you up to, Hope?" asked Faith.

Hope walked over to Faith and put her arm around her sister's shoulder. "Well, I wanted you to know how thankful I am for you. You helped me to the nurse's station today and you are always so caring. So, I wanted you to have this." Hope gestured toward Faith's bed.

"Your T-shirt!" exclaimed Faith. "Why would you want to give me your T-shirt? You worked so hard on it."

"I worked hard on it for you," said Hope.

"You mean you were going to give it to me this whole time?"

"No, not at first, but when I added the rubber bands I thought about how selfish I was for grabbing the medium T-shirt after you just helped me," said Hope.

"Then, I want you to have mine." Faith smiled, but then her eyebrows furrowed. "But what if you don't fit into my small T-shirt?"

"I can always turn it into a pillow or a scarf," said Hope.

"You're so creative!" said Faith.

"Thanks," said Hope.

"You know what? I'm thankful for you, too!" Faith exclaimed. She grabbed her new T-shirt and tried it on for size.

What Do You Think? ???

Do you have a favorite T-shirt? What does it look like?

_____

_____

_____

Were Faith and Hope thankful for each other in the beginning of the story?

_____

_____

_____

Why did they begin to appreciate each other more?

_____

_____

How can you overflow with thankfulness?
(Hint: Read today's verse!)

_____

_____

_____

_____

Style Tip!

✓ How do you know when it's time to wear a bra under your T-shirts? When you notice changes in your body. Have a good talk with your mom, and she will help you learn how to be modest when wearing fitted tees.

Try It!

Thankfulness Quiz

How thankful are you? Think about each example below, and then circle the answer that best describes you.

You notice your best friend is wearing the cutest T-shirt; you:

a. Ask her where she got it because you just have to have one.

b. Don't compliment her and think jealous thoughts all day.

c. Say "Cute T-shirt" and plan on shopping that afternoon.

d. Compliment your friend while being thankful for your own T-shirts.

During P.E. class, you realize you ripped your favorite T-shirt; you:

a. Ask to call home so your mom can bring you another T-shirt. You can't be seen with a hole under your arm!

b. Walk around for the rest of the day humiliated with your hand covering the hole.

c. Make jokes about it, but still feel embarrassed.

d. Are thankful you can ask your mom to sew it when you get home.

While sifting through a rack of T-shirts at the mall, you notice a T-shirt with a bad word written across it; you:

a. Think it would be cool to buy, and look in your purse to see if you have enough money.

b. Know your mom wouldn't like it, but want it really badly.

c. Shake your head in disgust, but still think it would be fun to wear.

d. Are thankful your parents taught you right from wrong.

You notice your T-shirts are getting too short and showing your stomach; you:

a. Think you are cool, hoping to look like a Hollywood celebrity.

b. Don't care if others see your stomach because that's the latest style.

c. Giggle as you look in the mirror thinking you look silly, but wear the T-shirt anyway.

d. Are thankful you have a little sister or a smaller friend to give the shirt to.

At summer camp, the counselors hand out T-shirts and you know the on they gave you is way too big; you:

a. Demand the right size because you don't want to look like a geek.

b. Pout, throw the T-shirt in your backpack, and don't say a word.

c. Hold it up for everyone to see, including the counselors so that they give you a smaller one.

d. Are thankful that you can sleep in it when camp is over.

If you circled mostly:

a: You care more about your appearance than anything else. Don't put so much pressure on yourself to be cool. Caring so much about what others think about you will only make you unhappy.

B: You keep everything bottled up inside. You don't care what others think, and you have a hard time complimenting others. You need to realize that God made you and you are special!

C: You try to make light of a situation, which is a great quality, but then you have a hard time taking that next step. Keep plugging away...you are almost there!

D: Congratulations! You are one thankful girl. You know how to be content in many different situations and are confident in who God made you to be.

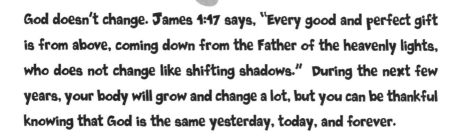

God doesn't change. James 1:17 says, "Every good and perfect gift is from above, coming down from the Father of the heavenly lights, who does not change like shifting shadows." During the next few years, your body will grow and change a lot, but you can be thankful knowing that God is the same yesterday, today, and forever.

Fashion Tip: Change it up! For a fun look, cut off the sleeves of a T-shirt, tuck a ribbon underneath each shoulder seam, and tie the ribbons into bows. You can add beads to the ribbon for extra pizzazz. Remember to ask for permission before you make that first cut.

Q: My friends and I love to wear T-shirts. Have T-shirts always been so popular?

A: Can you imagine life without the T-shirt? The word "T-shirt" wasn't even in the dictionary until the 1920's, and T-shirts weren't fashionable until the 1960's. Here's how it all started:

During World War I, American troops wore wool uniforms even on hot summer days in Europe. They noticed that the European soldiers were wearing lightweight cotton undershirts. The Americans loved the idea so much that by World War II, both the Army and the Navy wore undershirts as part of their uniforms.

Until 1950, T-shirts were thought of as underwear. Then, actors like John Wayne, Marlon Brando, and James Dean surprised Americans by wearing T-shirts on T.V.

In the 1960s and 1970s, people realized that you could make a lot of money printing on T-shirts. Professional bands and athletic teams were some of the first to sell custom screen-printed T-shirts. Everyone loved them and wanted to own a T-shirt with the name of a favorite band or team printed on the front. Later, companies put their logos, and artists put graphic designs on T-shirts, making the T-shirt a favorite fashion item for many.

Q: What can I wear with a plain white T-shirt?

A: There are many things you can wear with a white T-shirt to show your unique style. Here are some ideas:

Layer another T-shirt on top or wear a long-sleeve tee underneath.

Add decorations like buttons, glitter, patches, or rhinestones

Add accessories like a cool belt, a hat, or a pearl necklace.

Go with a black and white look by adding a black headband, earrings, and a black belt.

Pair your white T-shirt with a jean jacket for a casual look.

Remember to be creative and have fun!

Q: The favorite part of my wardrobe is my T-shirt collection. I have T-shirts in all sorts of styles and colors. My mom wants me to get rid of the T-shirts that are too small, or have holes or stains. I have so many shirts I can't close my drawers, but I want to keep them all. Help!

A: Each T-shirt is important to you because it reminds you of a special time in your life, like the vacation you took with your family, the school you attended, or the sports team you were on. You love your T-shirts because they are comfortable and cute, and they didn't cost a fortune.

But let's face it. After you've worn your T-shirts a year or two, they've usually gotten smaller on you and have a few holes and stains that just won't come out in the wash. What should you do with those old tees?

Try some of these fun ideas:

Donate your old T-shirts to an art studio as cover-ups for younger kids to stay clean.

Cut your old T-shirts into squares and sew them together to make a quilt.

Turn your old T-shirts into washcloths or dust rags.

Save your favorite old T-shirt and hook it over your desk chair as a decoration.

Fashion Fact:

In the 1960's, people began to tie-dye and screen-print the basic cotton T-shirt. The tank top, scoop neck, and v-neck T-shirts came into fashion shortly after.

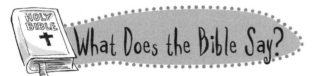

What Does the Bible Say?

Do you not know that your body is a temple of the Holy Spirit, who is in you, whom you have received from God? You are not your own; you were bought at a price. Therefore honor God with your body.

~ 1 Corinthians 6:19-20

Give thanks to the LORD, for he is good; his love endures forever.

~ 1 Chronicles 16:34

I will give thanks to the LORD because of his righteousness and will sing praise to the name of the LORD Most High.

~ Psalm 7:17

Enter his gates with thanksgiving and his courts with praise; give thanks to him and praise his name.

~ Psalm 100:4

✉ Letters to God

Hey God! I wore my cool tie-dye shirt home from camp. I couldn't believe Hope gave it to me. The smaller T-shirt fits her, but she'll probably only get to wear it this summer. After that, she has big plans to turn her T-shirt into a pillow or a scarf. I might do the same with mine once I outgrow it.

I had such a good time at camp, even though my hair turned green from all the swimming, and I have a couple of mosquito bites. Good thing Hope reminded me to spray myself with bug repellent or else I'd look like I have chicken pox. My mom would've freaked!

Hope and I made a good friend. Her name is Theresa and she stayed in our cabin. She's funny, and in the same grade as me. If it weren't for Theresa, Hope and I would have been late for everything. She is one on-time girl! And boy, can that girl swim. Her mom is right—she does live in the water!

The food was great at camp, too. It's not as good as my mom's cooking, but none of us got sick. We had eggs, bacon, and toast or pancakes for breakfast most days. Or we could have cereal. For lunch, we had sandwiches and fruit, and for dinner, we had hamburgers, spaghetti, chicken drumsticks, and fish sticks. Oh, and one night we made ice cream sundaes. YUM!

I have a lot to be thankful for: a great sister, a new friend, a fun time at camp, and a cool new tie-dye T-shirt.

Thanks God! —Faith

Now, it's your turn. Write your own letter to God and tell Him what you are thankful for.

T-shirt Pillow

As you make this T-shirt pillow, thank God for everything He has given you, like this T-shirt!

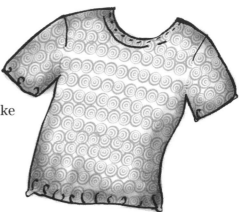

❋ What you need:

- ♡ T-shirt
- ♡ Filling
- ♡ A needle and thread or craft glue

❋ What you do:

First, pick a T-shirt. It is fun to use a favorite T-shirt that you've outgrown. Next, turn the T-shirt inside out and lay it flat on a table. Sew or glue the armholes and the bottom of the shirt closed. If you use glue, be sure to let it dry!

Turn the T-shirt right-side-out through the neck opening. Next, fill the T-shirt with stuffing, and sew or glue the neck opening closed.

Memory Verse:

Write down the memory verse from the beginning of the chapter. Memorize it. Think of someone you are thankful for and tell him or her today!

_____

_____

_____

Takeaway Thought:

After you've received Jesus into your heart, keep on reading your Bible and spending time in prayer. As a result, your faith will grow strong and you will be thankful.

Prayer:

Thank You, Lord, for Your goodness to me. Help me to be thankful in all circumstances because You care for me. In Jesus' name, Amen.

Chapter 9

Makeup 101

She speaks with wisdom, and faithful instruction
is on her tongue.

~ Proverbs 31: 26

Naomi's Makeover

Naomi puckered her lips and gently glided the strawberry lip gloss back and forth over her mouth. She not only liked the way her lips felt when she wore the shimmering gloss, but she also loved the way it smelled. Naomi rubbed her lips together, making a loud smack, and left the girls' restroom.

She joined her friends at recess. The conversation stopped when she walked up. Naomi looked at Maria, then at Carly. "What are you talking about?" she asked.

"We're just wondering when you're going to wear makeup," said Maria.

"What do you mean?" said Naomi. "I *do* wear makeup."

"You just wear lip gloss," Carly said.

Naomi didn't know if she was ready for more makeup. Lip gloss was fun. It smelled good. Why would she need anything more than that? Naomi noticed how both Maria and Carly wore mascara on their eyelashes. They even wore eye shadow sometimes.

After school, Naomi walked home and thought about what her friends had said at recess. *Does makeup really make you look prettier?* she wondered. *Does it really make you feel better about yourself?* Naomi walked through the front door.

"Hi," said Jennifer, Naomi's eighteen-year-old neighbor. "How was your day at school?"

Naomi didn't feel like she needed a babysitter, but her parents, who both worked every day, wanted to make sure someone was there to greet her when she got home.

"Fine," Naomi said. She slumped down in the overstuffed chair.

"You don't look fine," Jennifer said. "Are you tired?"

"Tired of friends," Naomi said, her arms crossed.

"What happened?" Jennifer asked, leaning forward.

"Maria and Carly asked me why I don't wear makeup," said Naomi.

"Makeup can be fun," said Jennifer, "but you have to be ready."

"What do you mean you have to be ready?" asked Naomi.

"Well, sometimes girls wear makeup to feel older," said Jennifer.

"I don't know if I'm ready," said Naomi. "But my friends want me to wear it."

"If you're not ready," said Jennifer, "don't wear it."

"But it might be fun to experiment," Naomi said. Her eyes lit up. "Do you want to help me?"

"Sure," said Jennifer. "But it's not good to share makeup, so we should get you some of your own. Let me call your mom. If she says it's okay, we'll go shopping."

"I'll go get my money, just in case." Naomi ran up the stairs.

"She said it was fine as long as I show you how to wear it," said Jennifer when Naomi came back downstairs. "So let's go."

They drove to the grocery store and looked on the personal items aisle. There they saw all kinds of makeup in a variety of colors.

"Why don't you pick out a few things while I find us a snack," said Jennifer "I'll be right back."

Naomi looked at the eye shadow and finally decided on a two-toned color in light brown since she had brown eyes. Next, she picked out mascara in black to match her hair and a blush in pink. She was deciding on a lipstick when Jennifer came back. "Wow, makeup is expensive," said Naomi holding a tube of lipstick in a bright red color.

"Yes, it is," Jennifer replied. She looked at Naomi's choice of lipstick. "Why don't you try a lighter shade?"

"Yeah, you're right," said Naomi. She found a pretty pink lipstick that reminded her of her shiny lip gloss.

The cost was three month's worth of allowance. "This better be worth it," said Naomi to Jennifer as they headed back to the car.

"At least it lasts for awhile," said Jennifer.

Once home, Naomi ripped open the packages.

Jennifer showed her how to put on the eye shadow and offered tips for clump-free mascara. Then, Jennifer added a small amount of blush on the brush and gently glided it on Naomi's cheekbones. Finally, Naomi put on her lipstick. "What do you think?" asked Jennifer.

"Wow, I do look older," said Naomi studying her face in the mirror. "It was fun to try this makeup on, but I still don't think I'm ready to wear it to school."

"I think you're making a good decision," said Jennifer.

"I think I'll call Maria and Carly and tell them," said Naomi. "I'd rather look natural, the way God made me. I do love my strawberry lip gloss, though."

What Do You Think? ???

Do you like to wear makeup? Why?

_____

_____

_____

_____

Do you think Naomi was wise in her decision to wait to wear makeup to school? Why?

_____

_____

_____

Which adults can you ask for advice before you wear makeup?

_____

_____

_____

_____

_____

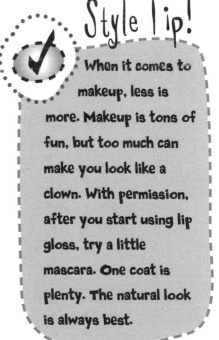

Style Tip!

When it comes to makeup, less is more. Makeup is tons of fun, but too much can make you look like a clown. With permission, after you start using lip gloss, try a little mascara. One coat is plenty. The natural look is always best.

Try It! Wise Crossword Puzzle!

There were twelve people in the Bible who were called "wise." Fill in their names to complete this puzzle. *Puzzle answers appear at the back of the book.*

Across

2. He was educated in all the wisdom of the Egyptians and was powerful in speech and action. ~ *Acts 7:20-22*

4. These men followed the star to see Jesus and worship Him. ~*Matthew 2:1-10*

5. Pharaoh made him ruler over Egypt and his palace. ~*Acts 7:10*

6. She was intelligent, beautiful, and because of her good judgment saved her household and later married David. ~*1 Samuel 25:3, 32*

8. The name of the advisor to the king who had wisdom like that of an angel and knew everything that happened in the land. ~ *2 Samuel 14:20*

10. The Israelites listened to him because he was filled with the spirit of wisdom. ~ *Deuteronomy 34:9*

12. He grew in wisdom and stature, and the grace of God was upon him. ~ *Luke 2: 40, 52*

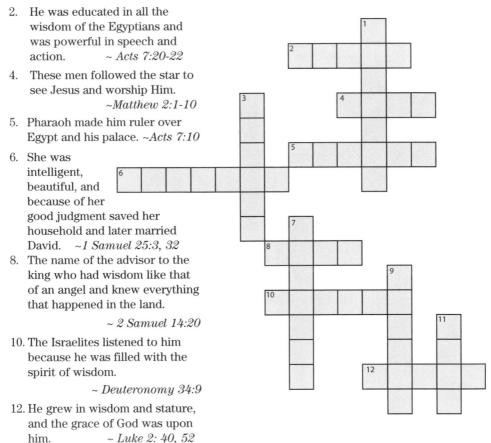

Down

1. He had skill, ability and knowledge in all kinds of crafts. ~ *Exodus 31:1-5*

3. He had knowledge and understanding, could interpret dreams, explain riddles and solve difficult problems. ~ *Daniel 5:11-12*

7. This king asked God for wisdom and discernment. ~ *1 Kings 3:5-14, 4:29-34*

9. The Lord was with him as he grew up and let none of his words fall to the ground. ~ *1 Samuel 3:19*

11. He wrote many books of the Bible with wisdom that God gave Him. ~*2 Peter 3:15-16*

Did you know?

Having a beautiful smile brightens your face more than makeup. Job 29:24 says, "When I smiled at them, they scarcely believed it; the light of my face was precious to them." You are so precious when you smile!

Fashion Tip: Brush and floss your teeth to keep them sparkly white. If you have braces, you can still have a beautiful smile. Try wearing different colored rubber bands for a festive look and make sure you have a toothbrush and toothpaste handy so that you can brush after every meal. Just think of the smile you'll have once those braces come off! Amazing!

Ask Kelsey!

Q: I've got the worst sunburn. My face looks like a raccoon's, because I was wearing sunglasses. My mom's not happy with me. She said it's important to learn how to take care of my skin before I can wear makeup. Help!

A: Your skin is the largest organ in your body. It helps protect you from infections and keeps you from getting sick. Your skin also keeps your body at the right temperature and allows you to have the sense of touch. If you don't take good care of your skin, you will be more likely to have a lot of wrinkles or even skin cancer, when you're older. Here are some ideas that will help you on your way to having the most beautiful skin on the planet:

❀ **Wear sunscreen:** Surprisingly, many girls don't think about sunscreen when they go outside. You should wear sunscreen with SPF 15 or higher when you go outside—especially during the middle of the day when the sun's rays are the strongest. And remember, every part of your body that is exposed to the sun needs sunscreen—that means your neck, and ears too. Hanging out with friends at the pool or the beach is fun, but having an awful sunburn when you get home is definitely not good for your skin.

❀ **Wash:** Your face needs to be cleaned twice a day with a gentle cleanser. While you're washing your face, you might as well hop in the shower and get the rest of your body clean.

❀ **Exercise:** How can exercise be good for your skin? When you exercise, you boost the flow of blood and oxygen to the skin cells, and when you sweat, your skin gets cleansed. So get your body moving. Run, dance, ride your bike, or do any other activity that will keep you active for an hour every day.

❀ **Eat healthy:** Food that is good for your body and skin is usually on the outer aisles of the grocery store. Fruit, vegetables, lean meats, milk, eggs, and whole-grain breads and cereals are examples of food that will help your skin look its best. Some great snack ideas are yogurt, peanut butter and celery, or whole-grain crackers and cheese. Foods like chips, candy, and soda are fun to eat, but should be consumed in moderation.

❀ **Drink:** You need eight glasses of water every day. Carry a water bottle in your backpack so that you can drink it throughout the day. Your body is made up of 60% water, so it needs all the H_2O you can give it. Your skin will glow!

❀ **Sleep:** As a growing girl, you need ten to eleven hours of sleep to keep those dark circles from appearing under your eyes. Remember to get your ZZZs!

Q. How come I have pimples on my face and some of my friends don't? What are pimples anyway? How can I get rid of them?

A. Your friends may not have pimples yet, but every girl gets a pimple every now and then. If you look real closely at your face, you will discover that your skin has tiny holes called pores. During the time you are growing and changing, your skin makes a lot of extra oil that might clog up your pores. A pimple appears on your skin when too much oil combines with dead skin and bacteria. As you look in the mirror, you may discover other bumps on your face as well. Whiteheads occur when a pore gets clogged up, closes, and then bulges out from the skin. A blackhead shows up when a clogged pore stays open and the oil appears as a dark spot. Some kids get what's called "acne" or a face full of pimples, whiteheads, and cysts, (deeper infections of the skin).

Nobody knows why some kids get acne and others don't. If one or both of your parents had acne as a kid, you might be more likely to get it, too. Acne can also worsen if you're under a ton of stress.

To get rid of pimples, follow these simple steps:

❀ Wash your face with a gentle cleanser twice a day, using your fingertips and not a rough washcloth. Don't scrub hard.

❀ If you use makeup, moisturizer, or sunscreen, make sure they are marked as "oil-free."

❀ Be careful when you use hairsprays or gels; they can clog your pores, especially around your hairline.

❀ Wash your face after you exercise. You don't want all that sweat to clog your pores. Gross!

❀ Don't touch your face. The oil and dirt from your fingers will only make things worse.

❀ Most importantly, don't squeeze or pick at your pimples. You don't want to end up with a face full of scars.

Having a pimple here or there is normal for a girl your age, but if you have a face full and it's bothering you, then it may be time to see a doctor. A dermatologist (skin doctor) can help you get your beautiful skin back. Hang in there!

Q: I can't wait to wear makeup. I play with it all the time and for my last birthday I had a makeup party with my friends. My parents won't let me wear it to school, church, or anywhere outside the house. Why not?

A: Your age may be one of the reasons your parents won't let you wear makeup out of the house. Right now, your skin is delicate and beautiful without makeup and you don't need to look older than you are. At this age, your eyes sparkle, and your cheeks glow—the natural look is perfect on you! If you still want to have a little additional color, try wearing lip balm, which comes in lots of different scents. It will make you feel like you're wearing lipstick and will keep your lips protected from the sun.

In the meantime, have fun playing with makeup at home with your friends. Find a fun book that tells you the correct way to apply beauty products like eye shadow, mascara, blush, and lipstick. And make sure you wash your face before you go to bed so that you don't plug up your pores. You're beautiful just the way you are!

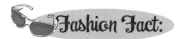

Fashion Fact:

Cosmetics (makeup) became a major industry in the 1920's and 30's. Glamour became an important fashion trend because of the motion picture business and famous movie stars. In the late 1950's, light shimmering lipsticks like the color Strawberry Meringue were popular.

What Does the Bible Say?

Set a guard over my mouth, O LORD; keep watch over the door of my lips.

~ *Psalm 141:3*

The mouth of the righteous man utters wisdom, and his tongue speaks what is just.

~ *Psalm 37:30*

For the LORD gives wisdom, and from his mouth come knowledge and understanding.

~ *Proverbs 2:6*

But God made the earth by his power; he founded the world by his wisdom and stretched out the heavens by his understanding.

~ *Jeremiah 10:12*

Praise be to the name of God for ever and ever; wisdom and power are his.

~ *Daniel 2:20*

And Jesus grew in wisdom and stature, and in favor with God and men.

~ *Luke 2:52*

Letters to God

Dear God, Last night I called Maria and Carly and told them I decided not to wear makeup to school yet. I thought they'd hang up on me or at least tell me they didn't want to be my friends. But, guess what? They said, "that's cool," and then we talked about other stuff.

The next day at school I asked Maria and Carly why they liked to wear makeup. Maria told me she likes to wear makeup because her older sister wears it. (I know Maria likes to do whatever her sister does, but her sister is sixteen!) Carly told me she wears makeup because Maria wears makeup. I'm glad I have a mind of my own! Carly also told me that she wants to be a beautician when she grows up. She loves hair and makeup!

Makeup is a lot of fun. I liked it when Jennifer showed me how to put it on. I wouldn't have guessed that Jennifer wore makeup. She told me that was the trick—to make it look natural, like you're not wearing any. I don't think I would have asked her to help me if she looked like she wore a mask on her face. Scary!

I'm glad that I've made a decision about makeup for now. I'm sure I'll need more wisdom for the next big decision in my life.

Gotta run. —Naomi

Now, it's your turn. Write your own letter to God and tell Him abou a time you made a wise decision.

_____

_____

_____

_____

_____

_____

_____

_____

_____

_____

_____

_____

_____

_____

_____

_____

_____

_____

_____

_____

Make It!

Fruity Lip Gloss

As you make this fruity lip gloss, pray that God will give you wisdom as you make decisions.

✳ What you need:

- ♡ Powdered juice mix
- ♡ Petroleum jelly
- ♡ Small container

✳ What you do:

Put ¼ cup of petroleum jelly in a glass bowl and microwave for 30 seconds. Stir the petroleum jelly until it is melted. Next, add the powdered juice mix to the petroleum jelly and stir. Microwave for another 30 seconds. Put the mixture in the refrigerator and let it cool. Once the mixture is firm, put it in a two-ounce container. Enjoy!

♡ Memory Verse:

Write down the memory verse from the beginning of the chapter. Memorize it. Think of a decision you need to make right now, and pray for wisdom.

_____

_____

❀ Takeaway Thought:

What happens when you are wise? Your tongue will speak what is right, and from your mouth will come knowledge and understanding. You will be able to make good decisions and give others faithful instruction.

🙏 Prayer:

Thank you, Lord, that You are wise. Help me to speak with wisdom. In Jesus' name, Amen.

Chapter 10

Sweaters & Coats

Be kind and compassionate to one another, forgiving each other,
just as in Christ God forgave you.
~ Ephesians 4:32

Abby's Sweater

"MOM!" yelled Abby at the top of her lungs. "MOM!" *I can't believe Catherine took my favorite sweater again*, Abby thought. She searched her drawers first, and then cleaned out her closet looking for the fuzzy pink sweater. She wanted to wear it for picture day tomorrow, and now it might be dirty or lost! "MOM!" yelled Abby again.

"Abby," said Mom, "what's the matter? You nearly scared me half to death."

"Mom, Catherine took my favorite sweater without asking—*again*," exclaimed Abby, putting her hands on her hips. "Now I can't wear it tomorrow for picture day!"

"That's what this is all about? I thought you had hurt yourself the way you were yelling for me," said Mom.

"Sometimes I can't stand having a little sister," Abby said. She shook her head and slammed the closet door. "Why doesn't she just ask if she can wear it?"

"I think she knows what you'd say," Mom replied, giving Abby a stern look.

"Of course, I'd say no!" Abby said, stomping her foot.

"Your sister is at a friend's house right now," said Mom, "but when she comes home, I'll have her talk with you. In the meantime, you need to calm down. How about some lemonade while you wait?"

"Maybe in a little while," said Abby with her arms crossed over her chest.

"Okay, come down when you're ready," Mom replied.

Abby sat on her bed once her mom left the room. She thought about her fuzzy pink sweater and how she felt when she wore it. She wanted to have the perfect picture for the yearbook this year, and now it looked like it wasn't going to happen. *Wait until Catherine comes home!* Abby thought to herself. *I'm going to tell her exactly what I think about her taking my favorite sweater.*

Abby's mouth watered at the thought of her mom's lemonade. She stood up and decided a chocolate-chip cookie would taste good, too. She glanced at the clock on her nightstand. Abby caught a glimpse of the picture her sister made for her yesterday. *You're the best sister in the whole world!* it read. A rainbow with fluffy white clouds made from cotton balls circled the words. Abby smiled at the picture as she picked it up. Catherine hid in her room for hours yesterday making the picture, and then surprised Abby with it. *How can I stay mad at Catherine?* thought Abby.

Abby walked downstairs. "There you are," said Mom. "You were so quiet, I thought you might have fallen asleep."

"I was just thinking," Abby said as she sat down on the stool by the kitchen counter.

"About what?"

"Well, after cleaning my closet, I noticed I've outgrown some of my clothes. If Catherine doesn't want them, I think I'll give them to the Rescue Center our Sunday school teacher talked about."

"That's a great idea," Mom said, and poured Abby some lemonade. "What are you going to say to Catherine when she comes home?" She looked at Abby with concern.

"Don't worry, Mom. I'm not mad anymore, but I would like her to ask me before she takes any of my clothes." Abby reached for the full glass. "And I'll just wear the purple shirt with my jean jacket tomorrow for picture day." Abby took a big gulp of her lemonade. "May I have a cookie?" she asked, smiling.

What Do You Think?

Do you have a favorite sweater or coat? What does it look like?

_____

_____

_____

What do you think Abby said to Catherine when she came in the door later?

_____

_____

_____

_____

How can you show compassion to your siblings or friends when you think they've made a mistake?

_____

_____

_____

_____

_____

_____

Style Tip!

What do you do if you have a small stain on your favorite sweater or coat? Depending on where the stain is located, you can always put a cute pin or an iron-on appliqué over the spot.

Word Scramble

Try It!

There are many different ways to stay warm. Unscramble the words below to discover a secret message. After unscrambling the words, write down the letter in bold. *Puzzle answers appear at the back of the book.*

__ __ __ __ __ __

CKJTEA

__ __ __ __

OTAC

__ __ __ __ __ __ __

ENSTT**M**I

__ __ __ __ __

AAKR**P**

__ __ __ __ __ __ __

ETWSARE

__ __ __ __

SEVT

__ __ __ __ __ __ __ __ __ __

EAWTHS**S**TRI

__ __ __ __ __ __ __ __ __

ISKACKETJ

__ __ __ __ __ __ __ __

NI**O**CTARA

__ __ __ __ __ __

ONHCPO

"The Lord is gracious and righteous; our God is full of

__ __ __ __ __ __ __ __ __ __."

~ *Psalm 116:5*

Did you know?

A little bit goes a long way when you give. Are there coats and sweaters in your closet that you've outgrown? Can you give them, along with the rest of the clothes that don't fit you, to an organization in your area that collects clothes for those in need? It will make you feel good inside and keep others warm.

Fashion Tip: On really cold days, layer your clothes. You can even wear two or more sweaters under your wool coat so that you won't have that itchy feeling.

Ask Kelsey!

Q: *My parents always want me to wear* a coat to school. The other day, it started out cloudy and cold, but then turned sunny and hot by lunch. While I was hanging out with my friends, I took off my jean jacket

...nd put it on the bench. I forgot about it until after school. When I went back to look for it, my coat was gone. My parents are going to be so mad. What should I do?

A: First of all, your parents want what's best for you. If they feel you need a jacket in the morning to keep you warm, then you should listen to them. But, you can also explain to them that sometimes you don't feel like you need your jacket once you get to school. Tell your parents about what happened. They will help you look in the Lost and Found at your school and notify the office of your missing jacket. During the next week, continue to look for your coat. Someone may have taken it home by mistake. It's best to put your name on all your coats, so that others know they belong to you.

Q: My grandmother knitted me a sweater for my birthday. When I tried it on, she twirled me around and had a big smile on her face. I don't want to hurt my grandmother's feelings because I know the sweater took her a long time to make, but I don't like the color. It's brown. If the sweater were pink, blue, or purple, then I would love it. Help!

A: I can tell your grandmother's feelings are important to you. Everone is drawn to certain colors, and chances are, the colors you like are the ones that look the best on you.

Here are a few color choices that would look great on you, according to your hair color.

Black hair—try wearing primary colors, such as red, blue, and green. White and black look great on you, as does bright pink.

Blonde hair—try pastel colors like powder blue, dusty pink, mauve, lavender, plum, and pale yellow.

Red hair—you will look great in brown, green, orange, and gold.

Brown hair—try ivory, bright green, red, blue, and peach.

As for your brown sweater, why don't you wear your favorite colored shirt underneath as well as a colorful headband, earrings, or a funky scarf? You'll look fabulous, and your grandmother will be happy, too.

Q: There is a girl in my Sunday school class named Anika who never wears a coat or sweater, even on cold and rainy days. I noticed her hair never looks combed and she wears T-shirts and jeans with holes in them. I did see her wearing a sweatshirt once, but it looked huge. The other girls don't like to talk to her, but I don't want to ignore her. What should I do?

A: You are showing compassion by being concerned about Anika and by wanting to do something about it. As difficult as it may be, especially in front of your other friends, invite Anika to sit by you. Ask her questions and get to know her. You may be surprised by what you learn. There may be a good reason why she dresses the way she does. Anika may need a little help in the grooming department and you may just be the perfect person to help her out. If it's OK with your parents, offer her one of your coats. Or, find out her size and shop at a second-hand store to get a good deal on a coat or sweater. Another idea is to get your friends together and have a fashion show with clothes they don't want or can't wear anymore. Tell the girls you are collecting clothes for Anika and that you would love it if they all would be nice to her. You can and will make a difference in Anika's life. You go, girl!

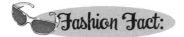 **Fashion Fact:**

In the 1940's and 50's, teenagers' clothing was influenced greatly by the American music and movie stars of the time. Girls wore knee length skirts with bobby socks, knitted shirts or sweaters, and flat shoes.

What Does the Bible Say?

The LORD does not look at the things man looks at. Man looks at the outward appearance, but the LORD looks at the heart.

~ *1 Samuel 16:7*

But you, O Lord, are a compassionate and gracious God, slow to anger, abounding in love and faithfulness.

~ *Psalm 86:15*

The LORD is good to all; he has compassion on all he has made.

~ *Psalm 145:9*

Yet the LORD longs to be gracious to you; he rises to show you compassion. For the LORD is a God of justice. Blessed are all who wait for him!

~ *Isaiah 30:18*

Yet this I call to mind and therefore I have hope: Because of the LORD's great love we are not consumed, for his compassions never fail. They are new every morning; great is your faithfulness.

~ *Lamentations 3:21-23*

Praise be to the God and Father of our Lord Jesus Christ, the Father of compassion and the God of all comfort.

~ *2 Corinthians 1:3*

✉ Letters to God

Dear God, As I was waiting for Catherine to come home, my mom handed me a laundry basket and asked me to get the dirty laundry from my hamper. I pulled out the huge pile of clothes and discovered... my fuzzy pink sweater. Oops! I can't believe I blamed my little sister. Well, I hugged that sweater and then tried it on. I looked at myself in the mirror and smiled. I imagined how nice my picture would look this year. Then a big chocolate milk stain the size of a quarter jumped out at me. Yuck. But then I remembered the cute heart pin Grandma gave me for my birthday last year. I quickly opened my jewelry box and grabbed the pin. I attached it to the sweater right over the dirty spot, and didn't even stick myself. Voila! Could this day get any better?

Mom called me just then and wanted my dirty clothes. As I gathered the pile and tossed them in the basket, I thought about the clothes I was going to give to the Rescue Center. I'm sure some girl would love my plaid wool coat. I'll have to put in a couple of sweaters, too, because wool coats sure are itchy.

That's it for now, —Abby

Now, it's your turn. Write your own letter to God and tell Him about a time you needed to show compassion to someone else.

Compassion Heart Pin

Showing compassion to others is sometimes difficult. When you wear this heart pin on your favorite sweater, it will remind you to show compassion.

✳ What you need:

- ♡ 2-3 inch wooden heart
- ♡ Paint
- ♡ Pin backing
- ♡ Rhinestones, glitter, lace, or ribbon

✳ What you do:

Paint the heart any color you want. Set it aside to dry. When the heart has dried, glue decorations on the heart. Make sure you don't overload it, as you don't want it to be too heavy. When the decorations are dry, glue the pin backing on the back of your decorated heart. Pin the heart to your favorite sweater when the glue is completely dry.

Memory Verse:

Write down the memory verse from the beginning of the chapter. Memorize it. Think about how you can show compassion to others.

_____

_____

_____

Takeaway Thought:

Being compassionate shows that you put other people's feelings before your own. You have the opportunity to show the people in your life how God would respond to them. Remember, God is full of compassion!

Prayer:

Thank You, Lord, that You are gracious and full of compassion. Help me to show compassion to others. In Jesus' name, Amen.

Chapter 11

All That Sparkles

Speak to one another with psalms, hymns and spiritual songs.
Sing and make music in your heart to the Lord.

~Ephesians 5:19

Selah's Big Audition

Selah played with her bracelet as she waited for her turn to sing. She knew she didn't have the best voice. Making the school choir would be a long shot.

"Hi, Selah," said Mr. Thompson, the choir director. "I'm glad to see that you're trying out for the choir."

Selah let go of her bracelet and hung her hands by her side.

"I would like to hear you sing *Jesus Loves Me*," said Mr. Thompson. "There will be no accompaniment, so you will have to sing acapella."

"That means no instruments, right?" asked Selah.

"Right," said Mr. Thompson.

Selah cleared her throat and stepped to the stage. She sang the best she could, keeping her eyes focused on the floor in front of her. After the song was over, Selah glanced up at the choir director.

"I'll post the list of choir members on the bulletin board tomorrow morning," said Mr. Thompson. "Thank you for trying out for Valley Christian's Choir!"

Selah gave a timid smile, nodded her head, and walked out the door. Her friends were huddled outside.

"I think Alexandra sings the best," said Julia.

"What about Natalie?" said Alexandra.

"She's a good singer too," said Julia.

"Hi everyone," said Selah.

"Oh, hi, Selah," said Natalie. "What are you doing?"

"I just finished trying out for the choir," said Selah. "Wow, I'm glad that's over."

The girls shook their heads in agreement.

"My mom's here. Gotta go," said Alexandra.

"Mine too," said Natalie.

"See you later," Julia said, waving.

Selah sat on the curb and fiddled with her bracelet as she waited for her mom to pick her up. She wondered why the girls left in such a hurry. She thought about the audition and her heart fell. She knew she couldn't carry a tune, but she did love to sing. At church on Sundays, Selah would sing at the top of her lungs as she worshipped God with her whole heart.

Her mom pulled up to the curb. Selah opened the door and hopped in.

"Hi honey," said Mom. "How was your day?"

"It was okay," said Selah. "I tried out for the school choir."

"Really?" said Mom. "How'd that go?"

"All right, I guess," said Selah.

The rest of the ride home, Selah looked out the window.

That evening she had a hard time concentrating on her homework. She thought about her friends and hoped to be in the choir with them.

Selah heard the phone ring. Two minutes later, her mom knocked on her door. "Come in," said Selah.

"That was Mr. Thompson," said Mom.

"Why would he call?" asked Selah.

"He wanted to let us know that you didn't make the choir," said Mom. "I'm really sorry, Honey."

Selah's eyes filled with tears. She swallowed the lump that formed in her throat. "But I love to sing." She wiped her eyes with her hand. "I know Alexandra, Natalie, and Julia will make the choir." Selah toyed with her bracelet. "You should hear them sing."

"Everyone is gifted in different ways," said Mom. "But God wants you to sing and worship Him no matter what kind of a singer you are."

Selah rubbed her bracelet between her thumb and index finger. She had made the bracelet herself. She loved to create her own beaded jewelry; she even made bracelets, earrings, and necklaces as gifts for family and friends.

"I guess I'll just sing in church, or when I take a shower," said Selah, smiling. "And do the things I'm good at, like making jewelry."

What Do You Think? ???

Do you have a favorite piece of jewelry? Is it a necklace, pair of earrings, bracelet or ring?

_____

_____

Selah did not have a good singing voice. Do you think that matters to God? Why? _____

_____

_____

_____

_____

What does Ephesians 5:19 say about singing and making music?

_____

_____

_____

_____

_____

_____

_____

_____

Style Tip!

The best way to take care of your jewelry is to keep it in a safe place. A jewelry box that has different sections for rings, earrings, and necklaces will keep your jewelry safe and protected. If you don't have a jewelry box, try making one!

Let's Sing!

Try It!

Unscramble each word below and place them in the squares to discover this hidden message. *Puzzle answers appear at the back of the book.*

"IGNS OT EHT ORLD A
EWN OGNS; IGSN OT ETH OLDR
LAL HET AEHRT."
~ Psalm 96:1

Did you know?

Birthstones have been around for centuries. In years past, there were many different sets of birthstones used, but over time the tradition changed so that now a single gem represents each month of the year. Birthstone jewelry is as popular today as it was in the past.

FIND YOUR BIRTHSTONE BY MONTH:

January—Garnet   July—Ruby

February—Amethyst   August—Peridot

March—Aquamarine   September—Sapphire

April—Diamond   October—Opal

May—Emerald   November—Topaz

June—Pearls   December—Turquoise

Fashion Tip: You can choose earrings, necklaces, rings, or bracelets with your own special gem. Are you having your ears pierced? Why not choose your birthstone as your first pair of earrings? You'll look adorable for six whole weeks while your ears heal.

Ask Kelsey!*

Q: I have this really cute heart ring that I love, but when I wear it, my finger turns green. Why?

A: Yikes! If you have a green stain on your finger, your skin is having a reaction to the metals used in your ring. Copper is a metal that turns the skin green. Your ring may have enough copper in it to cause a reaction.

All That Sparkles

Is your ring sterling silver? Sterling silver is 7.5 percent copper. The metal may cause your skin to turn black. Gold rarely stains your skin, but other metals like copper, nickel, and silver which gold is often mixed with can cause your skin to turn colors.

If your finger starts to itch and turn red, you are probably allergic to a metal in your ring. Here are some tips for minimizing allergic reactions when wearing jewelry:

- Look for jewelry that is hypoallergenic, which is best if you have sensitive skin.
- Put a layer of clear nail polish on your ring.
- Keep your skin dry when wearing your ring.
- Wear your ring only for short times.
- Keep your jewelry clean.
- Try wearing 18-karat gold or stainless steel for a green-free finger.

Q: I went shopping with my mom the other day. We have very different tastes when it comes to jewelry. I wanted long dangly earrings and she wanted me to get these tiny earrings that you can barely see. We had a big fight. What can I do?

A: You can find earrings in almost any shape, color, and design, but just like everything else in your wardrobe, it has to pass the "mom test." Your mom loves you and wants the best for you. It doesn't mean that she wants to treat you like a baby, but rather, to have you grow up a little at a time. The best thing you can do is talk with your mom. Tell her how you feel. Why are the long dangly earrings important to you? Do they match your outfit? Do all your friends wear them? Do you want to feel older?

Go shopping with your mom again. Instead of getting upset, meet her halfway. Find some earrings that dangle just a little bit. Take small steps. You want to look the age you are.

Q: I see some kids wearing skull necklaces, and belly button rings. I want to be cool but that look is not for me. How can I come up with a style I like?

The kids that you see wearing skull necklaces and belly button rings are trying to discover who they are, but they are going about it in a negative way. 1 Corinthians 6:19-20 says that your body is a temple of the Holy Spirit.

As God's girl, you can wear jewelry that shows who you are in Christ. If you go into your local Christian bookstore, you can find necklaces, earrings, and bracelets with symbols that represent the Christian faith, like crosses, fishes, or verses from the Bible. By wearing these symbols, you can let your light shine and possibly lead others to Christ.

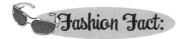

Fashion Fact:

In the 1920's, glass jewelry was made in large quantities. Fake, or costume jewelry was mixed together with jewelry that had genuine gemstones, for a unique look.

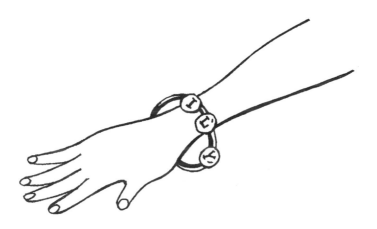

What Does the Bible Say?

I delight greatly in the LORD; my soul rejoices in my God. For he has clothed me with garments of salvation and arrayed me in a robe of righteousness, as a bridegroom adorns his head like a priest, and as a bride adorns herself with her jewels.

~ Isaiah 61:10

I will give thanks to the LORD because of his righteousness and will sing praise to the name of the LORD Most High.

~ Psalm 7:17

I will be glad and rejoice in you; I will sing praise to your name, O Most High.

~ Psalm 9:2

The LORD is my strength and my shield; my heart trusts in him, and I am helped. My heart leaps for joy and I will give thanks to him in song.

~ Psalm 28:7

You are my hiding place; you will protect me from trouble and surround me with songs of deliverance.

~ Psalm 32:7

O my Strength, I sing praise to you; you, O God, are my fortress, my loving God.

~ Psalm 59:17

✉ Letters to God

Hi God, This morning I had a hard time eating breakfast. I wasn't upset because I didn't make the choir. I was upset because I was going to miss hanging out with my friends. I thought Natalie, Alexandra, and Julia would have so much fun singing together in the choir. . .and I wouldn't be there.

When I got to school, I rushed over to the bulletin board. I saw Natalie and Alexandra's names right away. I scanned all the way down to the bottom. Julia's name wasn't there.

Then, I heard someone call my name. I turned around and saw Julia peeking out of the girl's bathroom. She motioned for me to come toward her. As I got closer, I noticed her eyes were all red and puffy.

She pulled me into the bathroom, and then leaned against the door. "Can you believe we're not on the list?" Julia said, blowing her nose into a wad of toilet paper.

"I'm not surprised I didn't make the choir," I said. "We both know I don't have the best voice, but I'm shocked you didn't make it." I gave Julia a hug.

An idea popped into my head. "Hey, why don't you come over to my house after school today and make some jewelry with me? We can play music and sing real loud."

Julia tossed her tissue in the trashcan. "If we can't sing in the choir, we might as well sing together." We giggled and then went to class.

Love, —Selah

Now, it's your turn. Write your own letter to God and tell Him about a time you made a joyful noise for Him.

_____

_____

_____

_____

_____

_____

_____

_____

_____

_____

_____

_____

_____

_____

_____

_____

_____

_____

Safety Pin Bracelet

As you make this bracelet, sing one of your favorite praise songs to God!

✺ What you need:

- ♡ Safety pins
- ♡ Seed beads
- ♡ Scissors
- ♡ Elastic thread 24 inches long

✺ What you do:

Open up a safety pin and slip on the seed beads—you can use a single color or create a pattern. Then, close the pin.

Thread the safety pin on the elastic thread with one end of the thread going through the top eyehole, and the other end of the thread going through the bottom eyehole.

Continue to put seed beads on safety pins and add them to the thread, turning every other safety pin upside down.

Carefully snip the elastic thread in half so that you can tie the ends of the top and the bottom lengths together to form a slip-on bracelet.

♥ Memory Verse:

Write down th memory verse from the beginning of the chapter. Memorize it. How can you make music to the Lord today?

_____

_____

_____

Takeaway Thought:

Did you know there are many songs created from verses straight out of the Bible? For example, Psalm 8:1 says, "O Lord, our Lord, how majestic is your name in all the earth." Do you know that song? Look in the book of Psalms to find a great verse and make a song of your own. Don't worry if you don't have a great voice; God wants you to sing from your heart.

Prayer:

Thank You, Lord, for worship. Help me to sing from my heart to You. In Jesus' name, Amen.

Chapter 12

In the Bag

I will praise you, O Lord my God,
with all my heart;
I will glorify your name forever.

~ Psalm 86:12

The Lost Purse

Ashley opened her denim purse and handed the clerk a twenty-dollar bill. She couldn't wait to see the adventure movie.

The ticket master handed her the movie ticket and her change.

"Thanks," said Ashley. She joined Katie and her mom at the door. They gave their tickets to the theatre worker before going to the snack counter.

"I'll go find us some seats," Mrs. Martin said. She handed Katie a ten-dollar bill and headed toward the theatres.

"Your mom is so nice," Ashley said. She inched forward in line toward the popcorn.

"Thanks," said Katie.

Soon it was Ashley and Katie's turn to buy their snacks. "Can I have a medium popcorn and a soda, please?" said Ashley to the worker behind the counter.

"Is that everything?" asked the teenaged boy.

"Yes," said Ashley.

"I'll have the same thing," said Katie.

Ashley looked at her watch. "We better hurry or the previews will start and the room will get dark." Both girls carefully carried their snacks and walked into the theatre. They looked for Katie's mom, but neither girl could find her.

"Let's just sit over here," said Katie.

It didn't take long before the girls realized they were in the wrong theatre.

"Let's get out of here," Katie said. She grabbed her soda and popcorn.

"I'm right behind you," said Ashley.

They looked at the signs more closely, quickly found the right theatre, and sat next to Katie's mom.

"What took you girls so long?"

"We went into the wrong theatre." Katie took a sip of her soda.

"The movie is about to start," said Mrs. Martin, dipping her hand in her daughter's popcorn.

The room turned completely black as the previews began. For the next two hours, the girls enjoyed the movie as they ate their popcorn, and sipped their soda.

"That was a great movie," said Katie as the house lights came back on.

"OH, NO!" Ashley exclaimed, jumping out of her seat. "I left my purse in the other theatre." A knot formed in Ashley's stomach. She carried all her favorite things in her purse: her wallet, hairbrush, and lip gloss.

"Show me where you left it," Mrs. Martin said. She followed the girls out of one theatre and into another. The three went up and down the rows trying to locate the missing purse.

"I thought we were sitting here," said Katie.

"No, I think we sat in this row," said Ashley.

"I'm sorry, Ashley," said Mrs. Martin after ten minutes had passed. "I don't see your purse anywhere. Let's ask at the front desk. Maybe someone has turned it in."

Ashley could hear the manager talking with Katie's mom. "No, I'm sorry. No one has turned in a purse," he said.

Ashley's hopes were dashed. Tears formed in her eyes.

"I always lose things," she said. "I just got that purse a couple of weeks ago from my grandma."

Katie clutched her mini backpack a little tighter.

"Time to go home, girls," said Mrs. Martin.

Once home, Ashley strolled up her driveway and opened the front door. "Mom, I'm home," she called. The house was quiet. Ashley looked out the kitchen window and saw her mom watering the backyard plants.

Just then, the phone rang. "Hello?" Ashley answered.

"Yes, hi," said a woman on the other end. "Is Ashley there?"

"This is she," said Ashley. "May I ask who's calling?"

"Yes," said the woman. "You don't know me, but I was at the theatre today and found a denim purse."

"That's mine," Ashley squealed.

Ashley wrote down the woman's name and phone number and promised that her mom would call back and make arrangements to pick it up.

Thank You, Lord, for helping me find my purse, Ashley prayed. She smiled as she headed outdoors to talk to her mom.

What Do You Think? ???

Do you have a favorite purse? What does it look like?

_____

_____

How did Ashley glorify God when her purse was found?

_____

_____

_____

How can you glorify God today?

_____

_____

_____

Style Tip!

✓ Your favorite purse may come from your mom's closet! The best thing to do is ask your mom if she has a purse she doesn't want instead of digging through her things without permission. You may be surprised. She may give you a purse you've had your eye on for years!

Did you know?

Purses, backpacks, and book bags come in all kinds of fun shapes, sizes, and colors. To keep your back healthy, you should never carry anything that is more than 15% of your body weight. For example, if you weigh 100 pounds, your bag shouldn't weigh over 15 pounds. A "backpack" style purse is best for your back.

Fashion Tip: Why not carry a wallet or a small purse? There are many purses to choose from that are small in size but big on style.

Ask Kelsey!

Q: My friend and I were talking about purses the other day. She says the most important thing is how a purse looks, but I say the purse has to be able to carry everything I need. Who's right?

A: You both are right. Girls have many different reasons why they carry a particular purse. The four most common reasons are how much stuff it holds, how many compartments it has, how easy it is to hold and get into, and whether or not it matches your outfit.

Whatever your reason for carrying a purse, here are several fun purse styles and ideas:

❀ **Tote bag**—these big bags are usually rectangular in shape and are perfect for carrying books and school supplies, or a beach towel and sunscreen. Totes are made from many different materials such as fabric, faux leather, or clear plastic.

❀ **Clutch**—a small bag that can carry a coin purse and your lip gloss. These purses usually come with little straps on the side and are fun to carry to church, a birthday party, or any festive event.

❀ **Shoulder bag**—bigger than a clutch, and smaller than a tote, a bag with a shoulder strap is the perfect lightweight purse to carry when you go to the mall.

❀ **Backpack purse**—a girly twist to the regular backpack, this purse is made for easy carrying, freeing your hands to do other things. These purses are roomier than most, can hold a number of items, and are perfect for every day.

Many girls own more than one purse, so it's easy to find the right purse for the occasion.

Q: The other day I caught my six-year-old little sister going through my purse. Doesn't she know that's my private stuff?

A: As long as you're not trying to hide anything from your parents, what's inside your purse is definitely your own personal stuff. Girls keep all kinds of important things in their purses, like house keys, wallets or coin purses, sunglasses, tissues, pens, hand lotion, hairbrushes or combs, and lip gloss.

Here's the thing. Little girls watch what older girls do and want to be just like them. Have you ever noticed your younger sister copying what you do and say? She looks up to you and can't wait to be your age. Talk to your mom. Tell her what's been going on and that you'd like your sister to keep her hands off your personal things.

Here's an idea. Why don't you give your sister a purse for her next birthday, or sooner? I'm sure she'd LOVE to have one of your old ones! Tuck a dollar bill in one of the pockets. Add a pen and a small notebook. Slip in a comb and a tiny mirror. Once your sister has her own purse, she'll be less likely to dig into yours.

Q: My parents gave me a brand new Bible for my birthday. I want to keep it looking nice. Is there such a thing as a purse for my Bible?

A: That's wonderful that you want to keep your Bible looking nice, but don't worry about how much you mark it up inside. Underline your favorite verses. Jot down a few notes. You'll be able to see how much you've learned and will be amazed at how much you've grown.

You can use any purse that fits your Bible, a bookmark and a pen, but there are Bible covers that are specifically designed for that. They come in all different materials and styles. Some even come with handles so they look like regular purses. You can find Bible covers of canvas, leather, or nylon at your local Christian bookstore, or on the Internet, but remember to ask permission to search.

What Does the Bible Say?

Glorify the LORD with me; let us exalt his name together.

~ Psalm 34:3

Because your love is better than life, my lips will glorify you.

~ Psalm 63:3

May the God who gives endurance and encouragement give you a spirit of unity among yourselves as you follow Christ Jesus, so that with one heart and mouth you may glorify the God and Father of our Lord Jesus Christ.

~ Romans 15:5-6

✉ Letters to God

Dear God, My mom was still watering the plants when I went outside to tell her about my afternoon. I told her about going into the wrong theatre, the fun movie, and my lost purse. Then, I told her about the phone call and the woman who said she had my purse. "Can you call her back, so we can get my purse?" I asked.

I followed my mom into the kitchen and listened to her phone call. "We'll be there in half an hour," she said.

I got a little nervous as we drove into the strange neighborhood. There were rows of small houses with bars across the windows. My mom drove very slowly as we looked for the house. We finally found it. It was pale yellow.

Mom said, "Wait here. I'll get your purse." She locked me in the car.

I watched as my mom walked up the cracked sidewalk to the front door. An older woman appeared and waved at me sitting in the car. Then, she handed my purse to my mom. They talked for a few more minutes. I saw my mom hug the older woman. They talked and laughed some more.

"You'll never believe this," Mom said as she hopped into the car and inserted the key. "That was my babysitter when I was a child. She's taking care of a sick relative," Mom explained. "I can't believe I found her after all these years." Mom smiled the whole way home.

So did I as I hugged my purse tight.

Thank You, God! —Ashley

In the Bag

Now, it's your turn. Write your own letter to God and tell him about a time you found something that was lost and glorified Him.

_____

_____

_____

_____

_____

_____

_____

_____

_____

_____

_____

_____

_____

_____

_____

_____

_____

_____

_____

Make It!

Denim Purse

To glorify God means that you want to worship or praise Him for what He's done for you. This denim purse will remind you to praise Him daily.

❋ What you need:

- ♡ A pair of old jeans
- ♡ Scissors
- ♡ Glue gun with glue sticks, craft glue, or needle and thread
- ♡ Ribbon 1" wide
- ♡ Velcro with adhesive backing
- ♡ Patches
- ♡ Fabric paint

❋ What you do:

Lay the jeans flat on a counter or table. Cut the jean legs off making sure to cut off all of the jeans inseam. Turn the top of the jeans inside out. Sew or glue the bottom of the purse closed. Let it dry.

Tie a ribbon on the belt loops for a handle. Add a favorite belt or ribbon around the waist for a fun look. Stick the Velcro inside the waistband of the purse so that it will stay closed. You can embellish your purse with fabric paint, or glue on patches. Enjoy!

Memory Verse:

Memorize the verse from the beginning of the chapter. Say it aloud to your Heavenly Father.

_____

_____

_____

Takeaway Thought:

The main reason to glorify God is because of who He is and what He's done for you. Did you know that God desires to spend time with you? He wants a relationship with you. He sent His son Jesus to die on the cross just for you. Spend time glorifying God today.

Prayer:

Thank You, Lord, for who You are and what You've done for me. Help me to take time to glorify You. In Jesus' name, Amen.

Chapter 13

A Good Night's Sleep

I will lie down and sleep in peace, for you alone,
O LORD, make me dwell in safety.

~ Psalm 4:8

The Slumber Party

"Girls," Mrs. Taylor said, peeking in Rachel's room, "time to get ready for bed."

Sarah closed the magazine the girls were reading.

"We're not ready yet," said Rachel. She jumped up from the floor. "We still need to style each other's hair, write in our secret diaries, and watch a movie."

"You can always do those things in the morning before Sarah goes home," said Mrs. Taylor. "Get in your pajamas and I'll make you some hot chocolate." Rachel's mom shut the door.

"Sounds good to me. I love hot chocolate," said Sarah, unzipping her duffle bag. She enjoyed spending the night at her friend Rachel's house. Rachel was an only child and the house usually seemed quiet. Sarah, on the other hand, was one of four children and her house always bustled with activity. "What kind of pajamas did you bring?" asked Rachel.

"My frog pajamas," Sarah said, holding them up. "I got them last year for Christmas. They are so soft and they help me sleep." Sarah rubbed them against her cheek and took in the clean scent of the laundry soap her mother used.

"Cute. Here's mine." Rachel pulled a nightgown out of her drawer.

"Pretty." Sarah felt a pang of jealousy as Rachel held up the silky lavender gown.

"Hey, you want to trade tonight?" asked Rachel.

Did she hear right? Did Rachel actually ask if they could swap? "Sure!" Sarah enthusiastically handed over the green and blue frog pajamas to her good friend.

"Girls, the hot chocolate is ready!" called Mrs. Taylor from downstairs.

"We're coming," Rachel called back.

"I hope I don't spill on your pajamas," Sarah said. She quickly undressed and then pulled the lavender gown over her head.

"Even if you do, don't worry about it." Rachel now wore the frog pajamas. "Let's go."

Following Rachel down the stairs two at a time, Sarah tripped on the silky gown and almost landed face first at the bottom before she grabbed hold of the banister.

"Hey, you all right?" Rachel turned around from the bottom step.

"Yeah, just a little embarrassed." Sarah caught up to her friend. "I'm glad I didn't rip your nightgown."

Rachel swung her arm over Sarah's shoulder. "Come on, let's go get our hot chocolate."

The girls laughed.

Seating themselves on stools at the counter, the girls slowly brought the steaming mugs to their lips. Two large marshmallows floated on the top of each cup, and touched their noses as they drank.

"Now I want you to go straight to bed after this," said Mrs. Taylor. "It's already 10:30 p.m."

"Okay, Mom," said Rachel.

"This is great hot chocolate, Mrs. Taylor," said Sarah. "I know it will help me sleep."

"Thank you." Rachel's mom smiled. "I'm going upstairs to bed now. Rachel, your dad is already sleeping, so go upstairs quietly when you're done."

"Okay Mom," said Rachel.

After fifteen minutes of drinking their hot chocolate and slurping down the marshmallows, the girls were ready for bed. They tiptoed up the stairs, and snuck into the bathroom to brush their teeth and wash their faces. Once that was accomplished, they walked quietly to Rachel's bedroom, trying not to giggle.

"I love your big bed," said Sarah. "I've never slept in a queen sized bed."

"There's room for both of us. Hop on in," said Rachel.

Once situated, Rachel turned off the light. It didn't take long for Rachel to fall asleep.

Sarah could hear her friend's deep rhythmic breathing. Sarah pulled the covers up under her chin. She tried to concentrate on how comfortable she was in the pretty lavender nightgown with the heavy comforter surrounding her body, but she didn't feel sleepy at all. She stared at the ceiling.

After what seemed like hours, Sarah noticed shadows dancing across the walls.

Then, a coyote howled.

She heard the wind rustling the leaves on the oak tree outside the window and the curtains swayed back and forth.

Sarah ducked under the comforter. She closed her eyes tight. She wanted to scream.

She missed her pajamas. She wanted her own bed.

Should she wake up her friend? Should she call Rachel's mom?

Sarah peeked out at the window. It was open. *So, that's what's causing the curtains to move*, she thought. Before she changed her mind, Sarah quickly hopped out of bed, ran to the window, and slammed it shut. She sprinted back across the hardwood floor and dove back in the queen sized bed.

Rachel kept sleeping.

Sarah settled under the covers. The bedroom was quiet. The curtains hung limp from the rod. She folded her hands together, and did what she should have done in the first place when she couldn't sleep. She prayed the simple prayer her mother taught her years ago:

Jesus tender Shepherd hear me,
Bless this little lamb tonight,
Through the darkness be thou near me,
Keep me safe 'til morning light.
In Jesus' name, Amen.

After saying these words, Sarah closed her eyes. Morning came before she knew it.

Do you have a favorite pair of pajamas? Are they made out of nylon, flannel, or cotton?

Why do you think saying a prayer helped Sarah go to sleep?

How can God bring you peace when you have a hard time falling asleep?

Style Tip!

It's important to wash your face before going to bed! Try making this bedtime mask for a clear complexion.

WHAT YOU NEED:

1 egg white

1 tsp. sour cream

1 tsp. grapefruit juice

INSTRUCTIONS:

Crack the egg and separate the white from the yolk. Put the white in a glass bowl. Set the yolk aside. Beat the egg white until fluffy. Add the sour cream and grapefruit juice. Mix everything together. Spread over your face and wait 15 minutes. Rinse off with warm water.

Try It!   P.J. Party

Have you ever had a Pajama Party? Well, here's your chance. First, you need to decide whom to invite. You can either make it a family event or invite friends.

So what do you do at a pajama party? Of course you wear your pajamas, have pillow fights, eat pizza, and watch movies…but you can also try these fun games.

Catch a Smile

Are you ready to laugh? This game is sure to bring a smile to your face. Have everyone sit in a circle. The person who is "it" starts out by smiling widely while everyone else keeps a straight face. "It" then wipes off her smile with her hand and throws it to another player. That player catches the smile and puts it on her face. Then, the new player wipes off her smile and throws it to someone else. Meanwhile, every other player must keep a straight face. One out-of-turn smile and you are OUT!

Noisy Charades

Write the names of noisy items (telephone, dog, motorcycle, etc.) on small pieces of paper. Collect them and put them in a hat or bowl. Select someone to go first. After she picks a slip of paper, have her look at the word drawn, and begin making the sound connected to that item. For example, if she picked "dog," she might make barking noises. The other players try to guess what the item is. The first person who guesses correctly goes next.

Did you know?

There are five different stages of sleep, including the REM (Rapid Eye Movement) stage, when your eyes move rapidly underneath your eyelids, your heart beats faster, and your breathing changes. Dreaming occurs during the REM stage, which follows the deepest stage of sleep. Scientists don't know why people dream. Some think it's the brain's way of sorting through what happened during the day, while others think you dream about what you are worried or thinking about most. During the night, you repeat all five stages of sleep at least four or five times.

Fashion Tip: Are all your pajamas in the wash? Don't worry. Ask your dad if you can wear one of his T-shirts, which is nice and big and oh, so cozy.

Ask Kelsey!

Q: I love to wear my nightgown to bed, but it gets all twisted up during the night and wakes me up. Help!

A: If your nightgown is affecting your sleep, then maybe it's time for a change. You'd be surprised at the huge selection of different pajama styles out there. When you go to the mall, look for:

Cami sets—camis with shorts are super girly and feminine and have spaghetti straps with built-in bras.

Capris—during the spring and summer months, you'll find pajamas in Capri style with drawstrings that let you cinch in the waist for a perfect fit. Add a matching T-shirt and you're good for a good night's sleep.

Tank tops with boxers—these are perfect for lounging the day away. But first, get a good night's sleep.

Traditional top-and-bottom pajama sets—these pajamas come in cotton or flannel and are perfect for colder months. Their long sleeves and long pants will keep you toasty warm.

Q: My parents make me go to bed at 8:00 p.m. every night. I stay awake in bed for at least an hour before I can go to sleep. Why do I need sleep?

A: Think about all the things you do throughout the day—go to school, play with friends, chores, homework, sports, youth group, and other activities. Wow! After all that, your body needs a rest. Your brain also needs to take a break. Sleep lets your body do that. Every child is different, but most kids your age need between 10 and 11 hours of sleep each night. If you haven't had enough sleep, you will feel tired, and cranky, and your brain will feel a little fuzzy. Getting enough sleep will help you grow and keep you from getting sick.

Q: The other night, I was just about to fall asleep when my younger brother came in my room and started talking to me in a weird language. Then, he turned around and went back to his bed. What was that all about?

A: Your younger brother was sleepwalking. Sleepwalking usually happens in the first few hours of sleep during what is called slow wave sleep or deep sleep. Studies show that 18% of kids sleepwalk regularly. Sleepwalking usually happens when a person is not getting enough sleep, is sick with a fever, or is stressed. Sometimes a scary movie, a test in school, or a bully on the playground can cause someone to sleepwalk.

When people sleepwalk, they don't see the same way they do when they're awake, but like your brother, they are usually able to find their way around. They don't remember sleepwalking once they wake up.

The best thing you can do to help your brother when he is sleepwalking is to tell your parents. They can make sure he is safe from any hazards during his sleepwalk. Sleepwalking is not usually a big concern, and your brother will probably grow out of it in time.

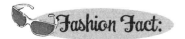

Fashion Fact:

For the last several decades, pajamas have been loose-fitting and designed for comfort, using soft materials such as cotton or luxurious fabrics such as silk or satin.

What Does the Bible Say?

I lie down and sleep; I wake again, because the LORD sustains me.

~ Psalm 3:5

The LORD gives strength to his people; the LORD blesses his people with peace.

~ Psalm 29:11

Peace I leave with you; my peace I give you. I do not give to you as the world gives. Do not let your hearts be troubled and do not be afraid.

~ John 14:27

I have told you these things, so that in me you may have peace. In this world you will have trouble. But take heart! I have overcome the world.

~ John 16:33

May the God of hope fill you with all joy and peace as you trust in him, so that you may overflow with hope by the power of the Holy Spirit.

~ Romans 15:13

Do not be anxious about anything, but in everything, by prayer and petition, with thanksgiving, present your requests to God. And the peace of God, which transcends all understanding, will guard your hearts and your minds in Christ Jesus.

~ Philippians 4:6-7

✉ Letters to God

Dear God, We had a good time this morning doing all the things on our "Sarah and Rachel's Sleepover" list. You should have seen the hairstyle Rachel made for me. I looked like an alien from a different planet. I had ponytails all over my head. I braided Rachel's hair into a gazillion different braids.

Then, we ate blueberry pancakes. I'm glad Rachel's pajamas are already a shade of purple, because a blueberry jumped off my fork and landed right in my lap. Rachel laughed. At least she wasn't mad at me. After breakfast, we wrote funny stuff in our secret diaries. Then, Mrs. Taylor let us watch a movie. We wrapped ourselves in our blankets and hung out on the couch.

I'm still a little sleepy from staying awake so long last night. I didn't tell Rachel that I was scared. I said, "Your bed is so comfortable," when she asked me how I slept. Her bed is comfortable....and big. I know the real reason I finally fell asleep was because I prayed. I felt safe knowing You were watching me.

I think I'll unpack my duffle bag now, and then take a nap, if I can with all my noisy siblings running around!

Love, —Sarah

Now, it's your turn. Write your own letter to God and tell Him about a time He filled you with peace.

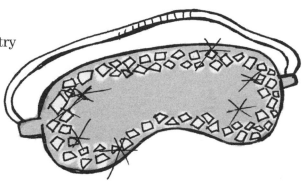

Make It!

Night Shades

Instead of worrying at night, try making this night shade so that you can block out everything around you and focus on God.

✻ What you need:

- ♡ Paper
- ♡ 9" x 12" sheet of self-adhesive black felt
- ♡ Scissors
- ♡ Satin material
- ♡ Hot glue gun
- ♡ 10" piece of black elastic
- ♡ Sequins, glitter, or fabric paint
- ♡ Craft glue

✻ What you do:

On the piece of paper, draw a template for the mask. Cut it out. Next, glue the black felt to the satin material. Trace the mask template onto this fabric and cut out.

Cut a 10" piece of the black elastic. Hot glue each end to the sides of the mask. Allow time to dry.

Finally, embellish your mask with sequins, glitter, or fabric paint.

Memory Verse:

Write down the memory verse from the beginning of the chapter. Memorize it. What does this verse mean to you?

_____

_____

_____

Takeaway Thought:

God wants you to come to Him when you are worried or afraid. When you pray, thank Him for what He's done in your life, and then ask Him for what you need. God will give you peace.

Prayer:

Thank You, Lord, that You give me peace. Help me to keep my mind on you. In Jesus' name, Amen.

Puzzle Answers

Hidden Word Puzzle

Page 29

BALLERINA FLATS
CLOGS
FLIP FLOPS
HIGH HEELS
LOAFERS
MARY JANES
RAINBOOTS
SANDALS
SLIPPERS
TENNIS SHOES

Z	L	O	V	S	L	S	Y	S	H	B	A	G	H	S
C	W	O	W	O	E	P	T	N	Y	E	O	Q	I	R
M	I	G	V	S	S	O	X	N	P	D	G	N	G	E
G	T	V	G	Y	O	L	H	W	I	Q	J	Y	H	F
A	A	O	E	B	E	F	A	S	V	H	M	A	H	A
O	L	Q	N	U	L	P	K	D	S	U	H	X	E	O
C	Z	I	L	S	X	I	P	D	N	I	O	A	E	L
O	A	R	X	K	N	L	J	J	I	A	N	P	L	O
R	P	L	D	D	S	F	K	O	H	U	S	N	S	R
S	R	E	P	P	I	L	S	R	N	T	H	Q	E	N
S	T	A	L	F	A	N	I	R	E	L	L	A	B	T
J	S	P	C	M	A	R	Y	J	A	N	E	S	J	T
U	Z	P	N	J	Z	T	T	Q	I	F	H	R	J	X
Y	U	L	Y	H	N	A	Z	E	B	B	D	C	L	T
A	A	I	G	B	J	C	Z	E	G	U	X	N	C	V

Outfit Count

Page 54
1) 6
2) 9
3) 18

Match—up!

Page 83

Baseball cap— cap with a visor

Beanie— a knitted cap

Beret— a flat round soft hat

Bonnet— a hat framing the face

Bowler— oval hat with a crown

Cowgirl hat—a hat with a high crown and a wide brim

Helmet— a hat of hard material

Sombrero— a Mexican coned hat with a very wide brim

Veil— a covering of fine fabric or net for the face and head

Visor— a hat with a partial brim and no crown

Word Scramble

Page 141

Jacket

Coat

Mittens

Parka

Sweater

Vest

Sweatshirt

Ski Jacket

Raincoat

Poncho

"The Lord is gracious and righteous; our God is full of COMPASSION."

~ Psalm 116:5

Wise Crossword Puzzle!

Page 126

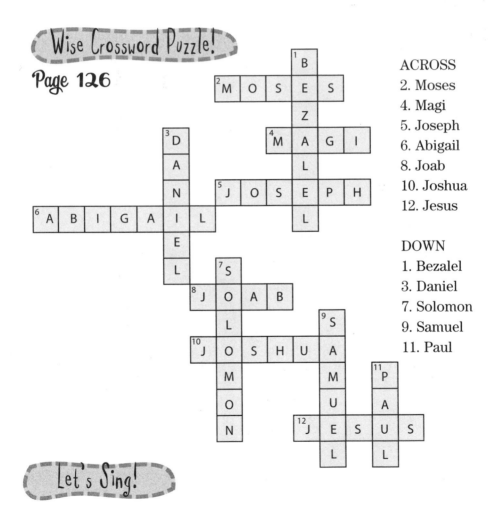

ACROSS

2. Moses
4. Magi
5. Joseph
6. Abigail
8. Joab
10. Joshua
12. Jesus

DOWN

1. Bezalel
3. Daniel
7. Solomon
9. Samuel
11. Paul

Let's Sing!

Page 155

"Sing to the Lord a new song; sing to the Lord, all the earth." ~ Psalm 96:1